Modern Baby NURSERY

HAND-MADE WITH STYLE

20 Crochet Afghans, Pillows, Wall Hangings and More • • •

LEISURE ARTS, INC. • Maumelle, Arkansas

••• Meet •••

KRISTI SIMPSON

Kristi Simpson enjoys designing cute baby gifts that mothers will love using. "There's just something special about having a handmade gift," she says. "It's personal and unique."

Inspired by her love of yarn, she creates crochet and knit patterns with a fresh and modern touch. The mother of five became hooked on crochet after teaching herself so she could help her daughter make a scarf from a "learn to crochet" kit that was a gift.

"I loved it from the beginning," she says. "I was amazed that I could take a string of yarn and create something so useful and pretty! Needless to say, I never stopped!"

Look for other Leisure Arts books featuring Kristi's designs at www.leisurearts.com/meet-the-designers/kristi-simpson.html. Visit kristisimpson.net or find her on Ravelry, Facebook, and Pinterest.

Introduction

Modern moms who love to decorate their nurseries and pamper their babies need to look no further than this crochet collection for inspiration.

Every nursery requires organized space for essential supplies and the Bunny and Storage Baskets provide plenty of trendy room.

Moms have needs, too. Rest with a pillow at your back and your feet on a plump pouf footstool. Fold that precious bundle into any one of three soft blankets or swaddle in a sweet cocoon.

Cover baby's toes with those cute booties and keep them warm and snug with the car seat cover.

Hang a banner in your nursery to welcome your new arrival or a mobile full of owls to engage the baby's senses. Little lambs are spotlighted in the wall hanging and the curtain tie. The bunny toy is just the right size for tiny hands while the rascally raccoon will be fascinating.

From fun to functional, you will find that special touch in soft subtle shades for your baby.

CONTENTS

Banner

EASY

FINISHED SIZE

Approximately 2¾ yards (2.5 meters) wide

GAUGE INFORMATION

Gauge is not of great importance; your Banner may be a little larger or smaller without changing the overall effect.

SHOPPING LIST

Yarn (Medium Weight) MEDIUM 4

[3 ounces, 197 yards (85 grams, 180 meters) per skein**]**:

- ☐ 2 skeins

Crochet Hook

- ☐ Size I (5.5 mm)

STITCH GUIDE

PICOT

Ch 5, slip st in fourth ch from hook.

BANNER

Ch 288.

Row 1 (Right side)**:** Working in back ridges of beginning ch ***(Fig. 1, page 77)***, sc in second ch from hook and in each ch across: 287 sc.

Note: Loop a short piece of yarn around any stitch to mark Row 1 as **right** side.

Row 2: Ch 3 **(counts as first dc, now and throughout)**, turn; dc in next sc, ch 1, ★ skip next sc, dc in next sc, ch 1; repeat from ★ across to last 3 sc, skip next sc, dc in last 2 sc: 145 dc and 142 ch-1 sps.

Row 3: Ch 1, turn; sc in each dc and in each ch-1 sp across: 287 sc.

Row 4: Ch 1, turn; sc in first sc, ch 3, skip next sc, sc in next 4 sc, ★ (ch 3, skip next sc, sc in next sc) twice, ch 3, skip next sc, sc in next 4 sc; repeat from ★ across to last 2 sc, ch 3, skip next sc, sc in last sc: 192 sc and 95 ch-3 sps.

Row 5: Ch 3, turn; sc in next ch-3 sp, ch 5, sc in next ch-3 sp, ★ (ch 3, sc in next ch-3 sp) twice, ch 5, sc in next ch-3 sp; repeat from ★ across to last sc, ch 1, dc in last sc; finish off.

Row 6: With **right** side facing, join yarn with sc in first dc ***(see Joining With Sc, page 77)***, in next ch-5 sp work (4 dc, work Picot, ch 1, 4 dc), ★ sc in next ch-3 sp, ch 3, sc in next ch-3 sp, in next ch-5 sp work (4 dc, work Picot, ch 1, 4 dc); repeat from ★ across to last dc, sc in last dc; finish off.

FRINGE

Holding 4 strands of yarn together, each 18" (45.5 cm) long, add fringe to each Picot across ***(Figs. 8a & b, page 78)***.

Booties

EASY

SIZE INFORMATION

Size: Small{Medium}

2" wide x 3{3½}" long
[5 cm x 7.5{9} cm**]**

Size Note: We have printed the instructions for the sizes in different colors to make it easier for you to find:

Small size = BLUE
Medium size = PINK
All sizes = BLACK

GAUGE INFORMATION

10 sc and 10 rows = 2" (5 cm)

Gauge Swatch:
2" wide x 3{3½}" long
[5 cm x 7.5{9} cm**]**

Work same as Sole on page 9: 32{36} sts.

SHOPPING LIST

Yarn (Medium Weight) 4

[4 ounces, 203 yards (113 grams, 186 meters) per skein**]**:

☐ Gray - 1 skein

☐ White - 1 skein

Crochet Hook

☐ Size F (3.75 mm)
or size needed for gauge

STITCH GUIDE

DOUBLE CROCHET 2 TOGETHER

(abbreviated dc2tog)

★ YO, insert hook in **next** st, YO and pull up a loop, YO and draw through 2 loops on hook; repeat from ★ once **more**, YO and draw through all 3 loops on hook **(counts as one dc)**.

SOLE

(Make One Each Gray and White)

Ch 8{10}.

Rnd 1 (Right side)**:** Sc in second ch from hook and in each ch across to last ch, 4 hdc in last ch; working in free loops of beginning ch ***(Fig. 3b, page 77)***, sc in next 5{7} chs, 3 sc in last ch; join with slip st to first sc: 18{22} sts.

Note: Loop a short piece of yarn around any stitch to mark Rnd 1 as **right** side.

Rnd 2: Ch 1, sc in same st as joining and in next 3{5} sc, hdc in next 2 sc, 2 dc in each of next 4 hdc, hdc in next 2 sc, sc in next 3{5} sc, 2 sc in each of last 3 sc; join with slip st to first sc: 25{29} sts.

Rnd 3: Ch 2 **(does not count as a st)**, hdc in same st as joining and in next 6{8} sts, 2 hdc in next dc, (hdc in next dc, 2 hdc in next dc) 3 times, hdc in next 5{7} sts, (sc in next sc, 2 sc in next sc) 3 times; join with slip st to first hdc, finish off: 32{36} sts.

On White Sole, place marker in Front Loop Only of first hdc made on Rnd 3 for st placement ***(Fig. 2, page 77)***.

Joining: Hold two Soles with **wrong** sides together, matching sts, and Gray Sole facing you. Do **not** begin with slip knot on hook. Holding White to the back and working through **both** loops of **both** pieces, insert hook in any st on Rnd 3, YO and pull up a loop, slip st in each st around; cut yarn. Remove hook from loop. Insert hook from **back** to **front** through center of first st, hook loop and draw through, YO and pull end through loop.

SIDES AND TOE

Rnd 1 (Right side)**:** With Gray Sole away from you and working in Back Loops Only, join Gray with sc in marked loop ***(see Joining With Sc, page 77)***; remove marker, sc in each st around; join with slip st to **both** loops of first sc: 32{36} sc.

Rnd 2: Ch 1, sc in both loops of each sc around; join with slip st to first sc.

Rnd 3: Ch 1, sc in same st as joining and in next 11{13} sc, working in Front Loops Only, dc2tog 8 times, working in **both** loops, sc in last 4{6} sc; join with slip st to first sc: 24{28} sts.

Rnd 4: Ch 1, sc in same st as joining and in next 11{13} sc, working in Front Loops Only, dc2tog 4 times, working in **both** loops, sc in last 4{6} sc; join with slip st to first sc: 20{24} sts.

Rnd 5: Ch 1, sc in same st as joining and in next 11{13} sc, working in Front Loops Only, dc2tog twice, working in **both** loops, sc in last 4{6} sc; join with slip st to first sc: 18{22} sts.

Rnds 6-8: Ch 1, sc in each st around; join with slip st to first sc.

Rnd 9: Turn; sc in Back Loops Only of each sc around ***(Fig. 2, page 77)***; join with slip st to **both** loops of first sc.

Rnd 10: Ch 1, sc in each sc around; join with slip st to first sc.

Rnd 11: ★ Ch 5, slip st in second ch from hook and in next 3 chs, slip st in next sc on Rnd 10; repeat from ★ around; ending with last slip st in same st as joining, finish off.

Bunny Basket

EASY

FINISHED SIZE

Base: 10" square (25.5 cm)

Sides: 8" tall (20.5 cm) with Brim rolled

GAUGE INFORMATION

10 sc and 12 rows = 4" (10 cm)

Gauge Swatch:
4" (10 cm) square

Ch 11.

Row 1: Sc in second ch from hook and in each ch across: 10 dc.

Rows 2-12: Ch 1, turn; sc in each sc across.

Finish off.

SHOPPING LIST

Yarn (Super Bulky Weight) SUPER BULKY 6

[12 ounces, 223 yards
(340 grams, 204 meters) per skein]:

- ☐ White - 1 skein
- ☐ Gray - 1 skein

Crochet Hook

- ☐ Size M/N (9 mm)
 or size needed for gauge

Additional Supplies

- ☐ Yarn needle

STITCH GUIDE

SINGLE CROCHET 2 TOGETHER *(abbreviated sc2tog)*

Pull up a loop in each of next 2 sc, YO and draw through all 3 loops on hook **(counts as one sc)**.

BASE

With White, ch 6.

Row 1 (Right side)**:** Sc in second ch from hook and in each ch across: 5 sc.

Note: Loop a short piece of yarn around any stitch to mark Row 1 as **right** side.

Rows 2-5: Ch 1, turn; sc in each sc across.

Row 6: Ch 1, do **not** turn; sc in end of next 5 rows: 5 sc.

Rows 7-10: Ch 1, turn; sc in each sc across.

Row 11: Ch 1, do **not** turn; sc in end of next 5 rows; working in free loops of beginning ch ***(Fig. 3b, page 77)***, sc in next 5 chs: 10 sc.

Rows 12-15: Ch 1, turn; sc in each sc across.

Row 16: Ch 1, do **not** turn; sc in end of next 10 rows: 10 sc.

Rows 17-20: Ch 1, turn; sc in each sc across.

Row 21: Ch 1, do **not** turn; sc in end of next 5 rows and in next 5 sc on Row 5; sc in end of next 5 rows: 15 sc.

Rows 22-25: Ch 1, turn; sc in each sc across.

Row 26: Ch 1, do **not** turn; sc in end of next 5 rows and in next 5 sc on Row 10; sc in end of next 5 rows: 15 sc.

Rows 27-30: Ch 1, turn; sc in each sc across.

Row 31: Ch 1, do **not** turn; sc in end of next 5 rows and in next 10 sc on Row 15; sc in end of next 5 rows: 20 sc.

Rows 32-35: Ch 1, turn; sc in each sc across.

Place marker in first sc on Row 35 for st placement.

Row 36: Ch 1, do **not** turn; sc in end of next 5 rows and in next 10 sc on Row 20; sc in end of next 5 rows: 20 sc.

Rows 37-40: Ch 1, turn; sc in each sc across.

Place marker in first sc on Row 40 for st placement.

Row 41: Ch 1, do **not** turn; sc in end of next 5 rows and in next 15 sc on Row 25; sc in end of next 5 rows: 25 sc.

Rows 42-45: Ch 1, turn; sc in each sc across.

Finish off.

FIRST SIDE

Row 1: With **right** side facing, join White with sc in end of Row 45 ***(see Joining With Sc, page 77)***; sc in end of next 4 rows and in next 15 sc across Row 30, sc in end of next 5 rows: 25 sc.

Rows 2-20: Ch 1, turn; sc in each sc across.

Finish off leaving a long end for sewing.

SECOND SIDE

Row 1: With **right** side facing, join White with sc in marked sc on Row 35; remove marker, sc in each sc across Row 35 and in end of next 5 rows: 25 sc.

Rows 2-20: Ch 1, turn; sc in each sc across.

Finish off leaving a long end for sewing.

THIRD SIDE

Row 1: With **right** side facing, join White with sc in marked sc on Row 40; remove marker, sc in each sc across Row 40 and in end of next 5 rows: 25 sc.

Rows 2-20: Ch 1, turn; sc in each sc across.

Finish off leaving a long end for sewing.

FOURTH SIDE

Row 1: With **right** side facing, join White with sc in first sc on Row 45; sc in each sc across: 25 sc.

Rows 2-20: Ch 1, turn; sc in each sc across.

Finish off leaving a long end for sewing.

FINISHING

With **wrong** sides together and using long ends, sew Sides together to form a cube.

BRIM

Rnd 1: With **wrong** side facing, join White with sc in any corner; sc in next 22 sc, sc2tog, (sc in next 23 sc, sc2tog) around; join with slip st to first sc: 96 sc.

Rnds 2-7: Ch 1, sc in each sc around; join with slip st to first sc.

Rnd 8: Ch 1, (sc in next 22 sc, sc2tog) around; join with slip st to first sc changing to Gray ***(Fig. 5b, page 77)***, drop White: 92 sc.

Rnd 9: Ch 1, sc in each sc around; join with slip st to first sc changing to White, cut Gray.

Rnd 10: Ch 1, sc in each sc around; join with slip st to first sc, finish off.

Roll Brim down.

BUNNY

BODY

Rnd 1 (Right side)**:** With Gray, ch 4, 11 dc in fourth ch from hook **(3 skipped chs count as first dc)**; join with slip st to first dc, finish off leaving a long end for sewing: 12 dc.

Note: Mark Rnd 1 as **right** side.

HEAD

Rnd 1 (Right side)**:** With Gray, ch 2, 8 sc in second ch from hook; join with slip st to first sc.

Note: Mark Rnd 1 as **right** side.

Rnd 2 (Ears)**:** Ch 8, slip st in same st as joining and in next sc, (slip st, ch 8, slip st) in next sc; finish off.

Sew Ears closed.

With **right** sides facing, sew Body to Head, then sew Bunny to one side of Basket.

White & Gray Blanket

EASY

FINISHED SIZE

30" wide x 48" long
(76 cm x 122 cm)

GAUGE INFORMATION

In pattern,
11 sts and 9 rows = 4" (10 cm)

Gauge Swatch:
4" (10 cm) square

Ch 12.

Row 1: Sc in second ch from hook and in each ch across: 11 sc.

Row 2: Ch 3 **(counts as first dc)**, turn; dc in next sc, (skip next sc, 2 dc in next sc) across to last sc, dc in last sc.

Row 3: Ch 1, turn; sc in each dc across.

Rows 4-9: Repeat Rows 2 and 3, 3 times.

Finish off.

SHOPPING LIST

Yarn (Medium Weight) MEDIUM 4

[7 ounces, 432 yards
(198 grams, 395 meters) per skein**]**:

☐ White - 2 skeins

☐ Gray - 1 skein

Crochet Hook

☐ Size I (5.5 mm)
or size needed for gauge

STITCH GUIDE

FRONT POST TREBLE CROCHET *(abbreviated FPtr)*

YO twice, insert hook from **front** to **back** around post of st indicated ***(Fig. 4, page 77)***, YO and pull up a loop (4 loops on hook), (YO and draw through 2 loops on hook) 3 times.

BODY

With White, ch 92.

Row 1: Working in back ridges of beginning ch ***(Fig. 1, page 77)***, sc in second ch from hook and in each ch across: 91 sc.

Row 2 (Right side)**:** Ch 3 **(counts as first dc, now and throughout)**, turn; dc in next sc, (skip next sc, 2 dc in next sc) across to last sc, dc in last sc.

Note: Loop a short piece of yarn around any stitch to mark Row 2 as **right** side.

Row 3: Ch 1, turn; sc in each dc across.

Row 4: Ch 3, turn; dc in next sc, (skip next sc, 2 dc in next sc) across to last sc, dc in last sc.

Rows 5-9: Repeat Rows 3 and 4 twice, then repeat Row 3 once **more**.

Row 10: Ch 3, turn; dc in next sc and in each sc across changing to Gray in last dc ***(Fig. 5a, page 77)***, cut White.

Row 11: Ch 3, turn; skip next 2 dc, 5 dc in next dc, ★ skip next 3 dc, 5 dc in next dc; repeat from ★ across to last 3 dc, skip next 2 dc, dc in last dc: 112 dc.

Row 12: Ch 1, turn; sc in each dc across changing to White in last sc, cut Gray.

Row 13: Ch 1, turn; sc in first sc, work FPtr around second dc 3 rows **below**, ch 1, skip 2 sc from last sc made, sc in next sc, ch 1, skip next 3 dc 3 rows **below**, work FPtr around next dc, ★ ch 1, skip next 4 sc from last sc made, sc in next sc, ch 1, skip next 3 dc 3 rows **below**, work FPtr around next dc; repeat from ★ across to last 3 sc, skip next 2 sc, sc in last sc: 47 sts and 44 ch-1 sps.

Row 14: Ch 3, turn; dc in next st and in each ch-1 sp and each st across: 91 dc.

Rows 15-30: Repeat Rows 11-14, 4 times.

Row 31: Ch 1, turn; sc in each dc across.

Row 32: Ch 3, turn; dc in next sc, (skip next sc, 2 dc in next sc) across to last sc, dc in last sc.

Rows 33-106: Repeat Rows 31 and 32, 37 times.

Finish off.

Chandelier

EASY

FINISHED SIZE

12" diameter x 10" long
(30.5 cm x 25.5 cm)
(excluding fringe and hanger)

GAUGE INFORMATION

4 dc and 2 rows = 2" (5 cm)

Gauge Swatch:
2" (5 cm) square

Ch 6.

Row 1: Dc in fourth ch from hook and in next 2 chs: 4 sts.

Row 2: Ch 3 **(counts as first dc)**, turn; dc in next 2 dc and in top of beginning ch, finish off: 4 dc.

SHOPPING LIST

Yarn (Super Bulky Weight) SUPER BULKY 6
[12 ounces, 223 yards
(340 grams, 204 meters) per skein**]**:

☐ 2 skeins

Crochet Hook

☐ Size M/N (9 mm)
or size needed for gauge

Additional Supplies

☐ 12" (30.5 cm) diameter wooden embroidery hoop (outer hoop only)

STITCH GUIDE

PICOT

Ch 4, slip st in fourth ch from hook.

BODY

Rnd 1 (Right side)**:** Join yarn around hoop with sc ***(see Joining With Sc, page 77)***; 4 sc around hoop, ch 5, (5 sc around hoop, ch 5) 9 times; join with slip st to first sc: 50 sc and 10 ch-5 sps.

Rnd 2: Ch 3 **(counts as first dc, now and throughout)**, dc in next 4 sc, ch 3, sc in center ch of next ch-5, work Picot, ch 3, ★ dc in next 5 sc, ch 3, sc in center ch of next ch-5, work Picot, ch 3; repeat from ★ around; join with slip st to first dc: 50 dc and 20 ch-3 sps.

Rnd 3: Ch 3, dc in next 4 dc, ch 5, skip next 2 ch-3 sps, ★ dc in next 5 dc, ch 5, skip next 2 ch-3 sps; repeat from ★ around; join with slip st to first dc: 50 dc and 10 ch-5 sps.

Rnd 4: Slip st in next 4 dc and in next ch-5 sp, ch 3, 4 dc in same sp, ch 3, ★ skip next 2 dc, sc in next dc, work Picot, ch 3, 5 dc in next ch-5 sp, ch 3; repeat from ★ around; join with slip st to first dc: 50 dc and 20 ch-3 sps.

Rnds 5-9: Repeat Rnds 3 and 4 twice, then repeat Rnd 3 once **more**.

Rnd 10: Slip st in next 4 sts and in next ch-5 sp, ch 10, ★ skip next 5 dc, slip st in next ch-5 sp, ch 10; repeat from ★ around; join with slip st to first ch of first ch-10, finish off.

FINISHING

Holding 5 strands of yarn together, each 34" (86.5 cm) long, add fringe to each ch-5 sp across ***(Figs. 8a & b, page 78)***.

HANGER

Cut 5 strands of yarn, each 34" (86.5 cm) long. Knot one strand around hoop at center sc of any 5-sc group leaving a 4" (10 cm) end; secure end.

★ Skip next 5-sc group and knot one strand around hoop at center sc of next 5-sc group in same manner, secure end; repeat from ★ 3 times **more**.

Holding free ends of all 5 strands together, make a 2" (5 cm) slip knot for hanging approximately 7" (18 cm) from ends; wrap yarn ends around strands below knot and hide ends in knot.

Car Seat Cover

EASY

FINISHED SIZE

28½" wide x 42" long
(72.5 cm x 106.5 cm)

GAUGE INFORMATION

With larger size hook,
14 dc and 7 rows = 4" (10 cm)
Each Square = 6¾" (17 cm)

Gauge Swatch:
4" (10 cm) square

With larger size hook, ch 16.

Row 1: Dc in fourth ch from hook and in each ch across: 14 dc.

Rows 2-7: Ch 3 **(counts as first dc)**, turn; dc in next dc and in each dc across.

Finish off.

SHOPPING LIST

Yarn (Medium Weight) 4

[7 ounces, 432 yards
(198 grams, 395 meters) per skein**]**:

- ☐ White - 1 skein
- ☐ Gray - 1 skein
- ☐ Pink - 1 skein
- ☐ Blue - 1 skein

Crochet Hooks

- ☐ Size I (5.5 mm) **and**
- ☐ Size H (5 mm)
  or sizes needed for gauge

Additional Supplies

- ☐ Yarn needle
- ☐ 2" (25 mm) buttons - 2
- ☐ Sewing needle and matching thread

SOLID SQUARE

(Make 16—4 Each Blue, Gray, Pink and White)

With larger size hook, ch 25.

Row 1 (Right side)**:** Dc in fourth ch from hook **(3 skipped chs count as first dc)**, ch 1, dc in next ch, ★ skip next ch, dc in next ch, ch 1, dc in next ch; repeat from ★ across to last 2 chs, skip next ch, dc in last ch: 16 dc and 7 ch-1 sps.

Note: Loop a short piece of yarn around any stitch to mark Row 1 as **right** side and bottom edge.

Rows 2-11: Ch 3 **(counts as first dc, now and throughout)**, turn; (dc, ch 1, dc) in next ch-1 sp and in each ch-1 sp across to last 2 dc, skip next dc, dc in last dc.

Trim: With smaller size hook, ch 1, do **not** turn; work 21 sc evenly spaced across ends of rows; working in free loops of beginning ch ***(Fig. 3b, page 77)***, 3 sc in first ch, sc in next 21 chs, 3 sc in next ch; work 21 sc evenly spaced across ends of rows; 3 sc in first dc, sc in next dc and in each ch and each dc across to last dc, 3 sc in last dc; join with slip st to first sc, finish off: 96 sc.

STRIPED SQUARE *(Make 8)*

With larger size hook and Gray, ch 25.

Row 1: Dc in fourth ch from hook **(3 skipped chs count as first dc)** and in each ch across: 23 dc.

Row 2 (Right side)**:** Ch 1, turn; sc in each dc across.

Note: Mark Row 2 as **right** side.

Row 3: Ch 3, turn; dc in next sc and in each sc across changing to Pink in last dc ***(Fig. 5a, page 77)***, cut Gray.

Rows 4 and 5: Ch 3, turn; skip next dc, 3 dc in next dc, ★ skip next 2 dc, 3 dc in next dc; repeat from ★ across to last 2 dc, skip next dc, dc in last dc; at end of Row 5, change to White in last dc, cut Pink.

Rows 6 and 7: Ch 3, turn; dc in next dc and in each dc across; at end of Row 7, change to Blue in last dc, cut White.

Rows 8 and 9: Repeat Rows 4 and 5; at end of Row 9, change to Gray in last dc, cut Blue.

Row 10: Ch 3, turn; dc in next dc and in each dc across.

Row 11: Ch 1, turn; sc in each dc across.

Row 12: Ch 3, turn; dc in next sc and in each sc across; do **not** finish off.

Trim: Work same as Solid Square: 96 sc.

FINISHING

Using diagram as a guide for placement and with bottom and top edges together, whipstitch Squares together ***(Fig. 9, page 78)***, forming 4 vertical strips of 6 Squares each, beginning in center sc of first corner and ending in center sc of next corner.

Whipstitch strips together in same manner.

BORDER

Rnd 1: With smaller size hook, **right** side facing and working across short edge, join Gray with sc in top corner sc ***(see Joining With Sc, page 77)***; ch 1, sc in same st, ch 1, ★ **[**(skip next sc, sc in next sc, ch 1) across to next seam, skip next sc, sc in seam, ch 1**]** across to last Square on side, skip next sc, (sc in next sc, ch 1, skip next sc) 11 times, (sc, ch 1, sc) in next corner sc; repeat from ★ 2 times **more**, **[**(skip next sc, sc in next sc, ch 1) across to next seam, skip next sc, sc in seam, ch 1**]** 5 times, skip next sc, (sc in next sc, ch 1, skip next sc) across; join with slip st to first sc, finish off.

Rnd 2: With **right** side facing, join White with sc in any corner ch-1 sp; ch 1, sc in same sp, ★ (ch 1, sc in next ch-1 sp) across to next corner ch-1 sp, (ch 1, sc) twice in corner ch-1 sp; repeat from ★ 2 times **more**, ch 1, (sc in next ch-1 sp, ch 1) across; join with slip st to first sc, finish off.

Rnd 3: With Gray, repeat Rnd 2.

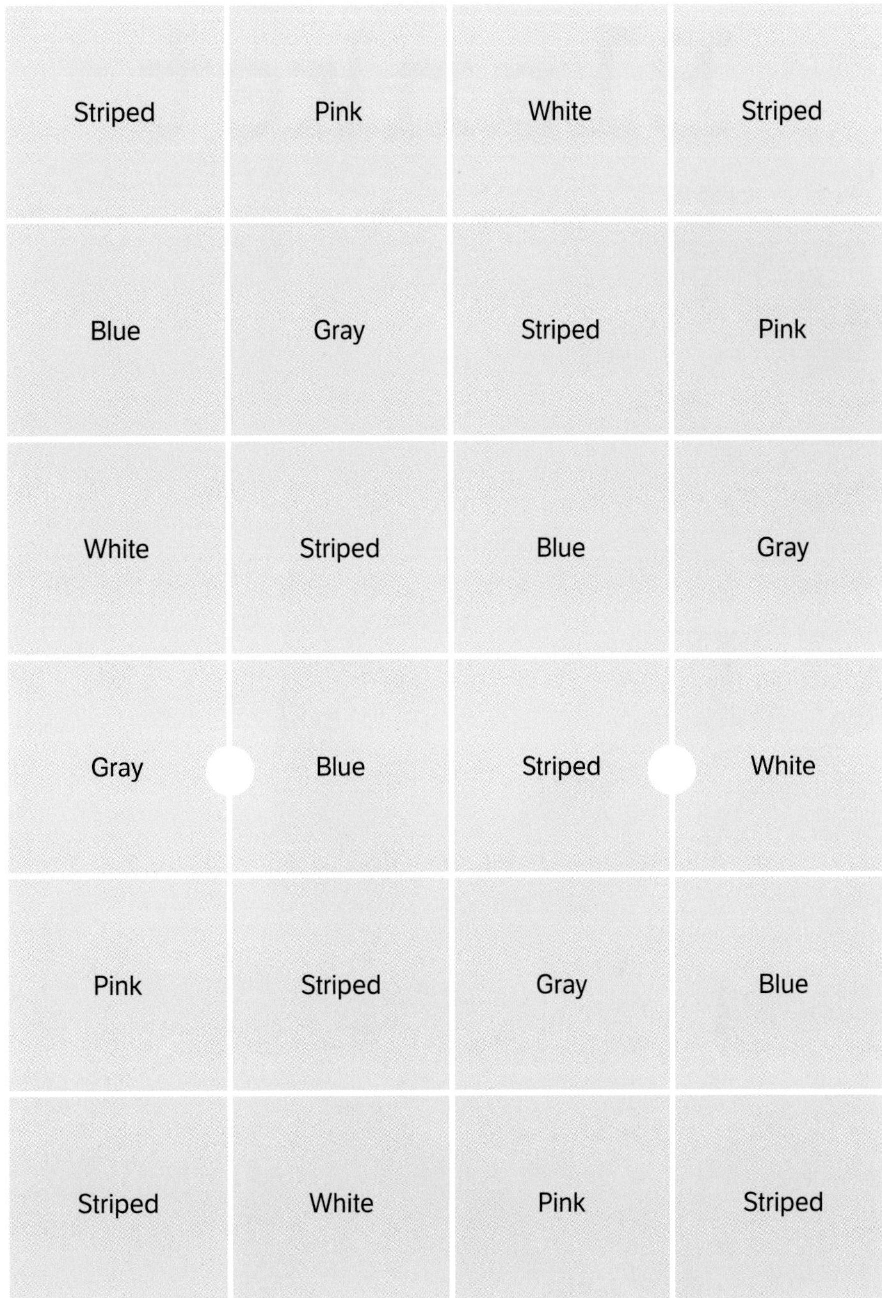

STRAP *(Make 2)*

With smaller size hook and Gray, ch 25.

Row 1 (Right side)**:** Sc in back ridge of second ch from hook ***(Fig. 1, page 77)*** and each ch across: 24 sc.

Note: Mark Row 1 as **right** side.

Row 2: Ch 1, turn; sc in each sc across.

Row 3: Ch 1, turn; sc in first 2 sc, ch 4, skip next 4 sc, sc in last 18 sc: 20 sc and one ch-4 sp.

Row 4: Ch 1, turn; sc in first 18 sc, 4 sc in next ch-4 sp, sc in last 2 sc: 24 sc.

Row 5: Ch 1, turn; sc in each sc across; finish off leaving a long end for sewing.

With **right** side facing, sew buttons to Cover as indicated on diagram.

With **right** side facing, button a Strap onto a button.

Thread yarn needle with long end and sew Strap to same seam above button, centered on next Square.

Repeat with remaining Strap.

Bobble Stripe Blanket

EASY

FINISHED SIZE

30" wide x 50" long
(76 cm x 127 cm)

GAUGE INFORMATION

12 dc and 6 rows = 4" (10 cm)

Gauge Swatch:
4" (10 cm)

Ch 14.

Row 1: Dc in fourth ch from hook and in each dc across: 12 sts.

Rows 2-6: Ch 3 **(counts as first dc)**, turn; dc in next dc and in each st across.

Finish off.

SHOPPING LIST

Yarn (Medium Weight) MEDIUM 4

[3.5 ounces, 210 yards
(100 grams, 192 meters) per skein**]**:

- ☐ Blue - 5 skeins
- ☐ Aran - 1 skein

Crochet Hook

- ☐ Size J (6 mm)
  or size needed for gauge

STITCH GUIDE

BOBBLE (uses one dc)

★ YO, insert hook in dc indicated, YO and pull up loop; repeat from ★ 3 times **more**, YO and draw through all 9 loops on hook.

BODY

With Blue, ch 85.

Row 1 (Right side)**:** Dc in fourth ch from hook and in each ch across **(3 skipped chs count as first dc)**: 83 dc.

Note: Loop a short piece of yarn around any stitch to mark Row 1 as **right** side.

Row 2: Ch 3 **(counts as first dc, now and throughout)**, turn; dc in next dc and in each dc across.

Row 3: Ch 1, turn; sc in each dc across.

Row 4: Ch 4 **(counts as first dc plus ch 1, now and throughout)**, turn; skip next sc, dc in next sc, ★ ch 1, skip next sc, dc in next sc; repeat from ★ across: 42 dc and 41 ch-1 sps.

Row 5: Ch 1, turn; sc in first dc and in next ch-1 sp and each dc across: 83 sc.

Rows 6-8: Ch 3, turn; dc in next st and in each st across.

Row 9: Ch 1, turn; sc in each dc across.

Rows 10 and 11: Repeat Rows 4 and 5: 83 sc.

Rows 12-14: Ch 3, turn; dc in next st and in each st across.

Row 15: Ch 1, turn; sc in each dc across.

Rows 16 and 17: Repeat Rows 4 and 5: 83 sc.

Row 18: Ch 3, turn; dc in next sc and in each sc across.

Row 19: Ch 3, turn; dc in next dc and in each dc across changing to Aran in last dc ***(Fig. 5a, page 77)***, cut Blue.

Row 20: Ch 2 **(does not count as a st)**, turn; hdc in first 2 dc, ★ work Bobble in next dc, hdc in next 2 dc; repeat from ★ across changing to Blue in last hdc, cut Aran: 56 hdc and 27 Bobbles.

Rows 21 and 22: Ch 3, turn; dc in next st and in each st across: 83 dc.

Rows 23-100: Repeat Rows 3-22, 3 times; then repeat Rows 3-18 once **more**.

Row 101: Ch 3, turn; dc in next dc and in each dc across; do **not** finish off.

BORDER

Rnd 1: Ch 1, do **not** turn; work 162 sc evenly spaced across ends of rows; working in free loops of beginning ch ***(Fig. 3b, page 77)***, 3 sc in first ch, sc in next 81 chs, 3 sc in next ch; work 162 sc evenly spaced across ends of rows; 3 sc in first dc, sc in each dc across to last dc, 3 sc in last dc; join with slip st to first sc: 498 sc.

Rnd 2: Ch 1, sc in each sc around working 3 sc in center sc of each corner 3-sc group; join with slip st to first sc: 506 sc.

Rnd 3: Slip st in next sc, ch 4 **(counts as first dc plus ch 1)**, skip next sc, ★ (dc in next sc, ch 1, skip next sc) across to next corner sc, (dc, ch 1) twice in corner sc, skip next sc; repeat from ★ 3 times **more**, join with slip st to first dc.

Rnd 4: Ch 1, sc in same st as joining and in each dc and each ch-1 sp around working 3 sc in each corner ch-1 sp; join with slip st to first sc, finish off.

Storage Basket

EASY

FINISHED SIZE

17" wide x 12" high
(43 cm x 30.5 cm)

GAUGE INFORMATION

7 dc and 5 rows = 4" (10 cm)

Gauge Swatch:
4" (10 cm) square

Ch 9.

Row 1: Dc in fourth ch from hook and in each ch across **(3 skipped chs count as first dc)**: 7 dc.

Rows 2-5: Ch 3 **(counts as first dc)**, turn; dc in next dc and in each dc across.

Finish off.

SHOPPING LIST

Yarn (Super Bulky Weight) SUPER BULKY 6

[6 ounces, 74 yards
(170 grams, 68 meters) per skein**]**:

☐ 6 skeins

Crochet Hook

☐ Size M/N (9 mm)
or size needed for gauge

STITCH GUIDE

FRONT POST DOUBLE CROCHET *(abbreviated FPdc)*

YO, insert hook from **front** to **back** around post of st indicated ***(Fig. 4, page 77)***, YO and pull up a loop (3 loops on hook), (YO and draw through 2 loops on hook) twice.

SINGLE CROCHET 2 TOGETHER *(abbreviated sc2tog)*

Pull up a loop in each of next 2 sc, YO and draw through all 3 loops on hook **(counts as one sc)**.

BASKET

Rnd 1 (Right side)**:** Ch 4, 8 dc in fourth ch from hook; join with slip st to first dc: 8 dc.

Rnds 2 and 3: Ch 2 **(does not count as a st, now and throughout)**, 2 dc in same st as joining and in each dc around; join with slip st to first dc: 32 dc.

Rnd 4: Ch 2, dc in same st as joining, 2 dc in next dc, (dc in next dc, 2 dc in next dc) around; join with slip st to first dc: 48 dc.

Rnd 5: Ch 2, dc in same st as joining and in next dc, 2 dc in next dc, (dc in next 2 dc, 2 dc in next dc) around; join with slip st to first dc: 64 dc.

Rnd 6: Ch 2, dc in same st as joining and in next 6 dc, 2 dc in next dc, (dc in next 7 dc, 2 dc in next dc) around; join with slip st to first dc: 72 dc.

Rnd 7: Ch 2, dc in same st as joining and in each dc around; join with slip st to first dc.

Rnd 8: Ch 2, dc in same st as joining and in next 7 dc, 2 dc in next dc, (dc in next 8 dc, 2 dc in next dc) around; join with slip st to first dc: 80 dc.

Rnd 9: Ch 2, dc in Back Loop Only of same st as joining and each dc around ***(Fig. 2, page 77)***; join with slip st to **both** loops of first dc.

Rnd 10: Ch 2, working in both loops, dc in same st as joining and in next 2 dc, work FPdc around next dc, (dc in next 3 dc, work FPdc around next dc) around; join with slip st to first dc.

Rnd 11: Ch 2, dc in same st as joining and in each st around; join with slip st to first dc.

Rnd 12: Ch 2, dc in same st as joining, work FPdc around next dc, (dc in next 3 dc, work FPdc around next dc) around to last 2 dc, dc in last 2 dc; join with slip st to first dc.

Rnd 13: Ch 2, dc in same st as joining and in each st around; join with slip st to first dc.

Rnds 14-18: Repeat Rnds 10-13 once, then repeat Rnd 10 once **more**.

Rnd 19: Ch 2, dc in same st as joining and in next 4 sts, ch 10 (handle), skip next 10 sts, dc in next 30 sts, ch 10 (handle), skip next 10 sts, dc in last 25 sts; join with slip st to first dc: 60 dc and 2 ch-10 sps.

Rnd 20: Ch 1, sc in same st as joining and in next 4 dc, sc in back ridge of next 10 chs ***(Fig. 1, page 77)***, sc in next 30 dc, sc in back ridge of next chs, sc in last 25 dc; join with slip st to first sc: 80 sc.

Rnd 21: Ch 1, sc in same st as joining and in next 7 sc, sc2tog, (sc in next 8 sc, sc2tog) around; join with slip st to first sc: 72 sc.

Rnd 22: Ch 1, sc in same st as joining and in each sc around; join with slip st to first sc.

Rnd 23: Ch 1, working from **left** to **right**, work reverse sc in each sc around ***(Figs. 11a-d, page 79)***; join with slip st to first st, finish off.

Pillow

EASY

FINISHED SIZE

13½" x 18"
(34.5 cm x 45.5 cm)

GAUGE INFORMATION

In Front pattern, 3 Shells and 6 rows = 4" (10 cm)

Gauge Swatch:
4½" x 4"
(11.5 cm x 10 cm)

Ch 17.

Rows 1-6: Work same as Front on page 34: 2 Shells and 2 3-dc groups.

Finish off.

SHOPPING LIST

Yarn (Bulky Weight) 5 BULKY
[5.3 ounces, 312 yards
(150 grams, 285 meters) per skein**]**:

- ☐ 2 skeins

Crochet Hook

- ☐ Size H (5 mm)
or size needed for gauge

Additional Supplies

- ☐ Yarn needle
- ☐ 12" x 16" (30.5 cm x 40.5 cm) pillow form

STITCH GUIDE

SHELL (uses one st or sp)
(2 Dc, work Picot, 2 dc) in st or sp indicated.

PICOT
Ch 5, slip st in fifth ch from hook.

FRONT

Ch 53.

Row 1 (Right side)**:** Work Shell in sixth ch from hook **(first 3 skipped chs count as first dc)**, ★ skip next 3 chs, work Shell in next ch; repeat from ★ across to last 3 chs, skip next 2 chs, dc in last ch: 12 Shells.

Note: Loop a short piece of yarn around any stitch to mark Row 1 as **right** side.

Row 2: Ch 3 **(counts as first dc, now and throughout)**, turn; 2 dc in first dc, skip next Shell, work Shell in sp **before** next Shell ***(Fig. 6, page 78)***, ★ skip next Shell, work Shell in sp **before** next Shell; repeat from ★ across to last Shell, skip last Shell, 3 dc in last dc: 11 Shells and 2 3-dc groups.

Row 3: Ch 3, turn; skip first 3 dc, work Shell in sp **before** next Shell, ★ skip next Shell, work Shell in sp **before** next Shell; repeat from ★ across to last Shell, skip last Shell, work Shell in sp **before** last 3-dc group, skip next 2 dc, dc in last dc: 12 Shells.

Row 4: Ch 3, turn; 2 dc in first dc, ★ skip next Shell, work Shell in sp **before** next Shell; repeat from ★ across to last Shell, skip last Shell, 3 dc in last dc: 11 Shells and 2 3-dc groups.

Rows 5-23: Repeat Rows 3 and 4, 9 times; then repeat Row 3 once **more**.

Finish off.

BACK

Ch 55.

Row 1 (Wrong side)**:** Sc in second ch from hook, dc in next ch, (sc in next ch, dc in next ch) across: 54 sts.

Note: Mark **back** of any st on Row 1 as **right** side.

Rows 2-26: Ch 1, turn; sc in first dc, dc in next sc, (sc in next dc, dc in next sc) across.

FINISHING

With **wrong** sides and beginning ch edges together, sew Front and Back together, inserting pillow form before closing.

Pouf Footstool

EASY

FINISHED SIZE

14" (35.5 cm) high

GAUGE INFORMATION

In pattern, 6 sts and 4 rnds = 3" (7.5 cm)

Gauge Swatch:
3" (7.5 cm) diameter

Work same as Body on page 37 through Rnd 2: 18 hdc.

SHOPPING LIST

Yarn (Super Bulky Weight) SUPER BULKY 6

[5 ounces, 125 yards (142 grams, 114 meters) per skein]:

☐ 5 skeins

Crochet Hook

☐ Size M/N (9 mm)
or size needed for gauge

Additional Supplies

☐ Polyester fiberfill - 30 ounces (850 grams)

STITCH GUIDE

HALF DOUBLE CROCHET 2 TOGETHER

(abbreviated hdc2tog)

★ YO and insert hook in **next** st, YO and pull up a loop; repeat from ★ once **more**, YO and draw through 5 loops on hook **(counts as one hdc)**.

BODY

Rnd 1 (Right side)**:** Ch 2, 9 hdc in second ch from hook; do **not** join, place marker to indicate beginning of rnd ***(see Markers, page 77)***: 9 hdc.

Work in horizontal bar of hdc throughout ***(Fig. A, shown from wrong side)***.

Fig. A

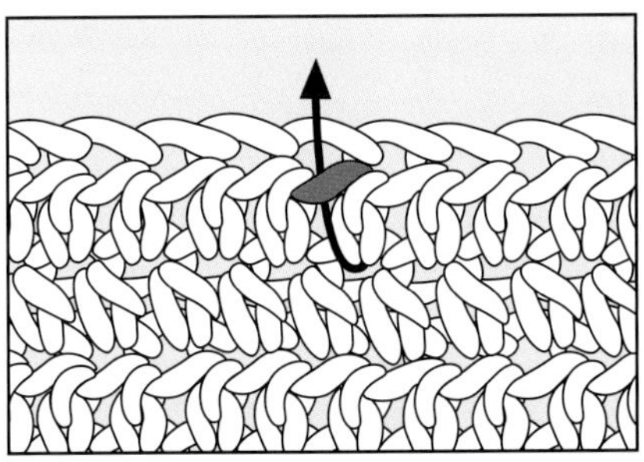

Rnd 2: 2 Hdc in each hdc around: 18 hdc.

Rnd 3: (Hdc in next hdc, 2 hdc in next hdc) around: 27 hdc.

Rnd 4: (Hdc in next 2 hdc, 2 hdc in next hdc) around: 36 hdc.

Rnd 5: (Hdc in next 3 hdc, 2 hdc in next hdc) around: 45 hdc.

Rnd 6: (Hdc in next 4 hdc, 2 hdc in next hdc) around: 54 hdc.

Rnd 7: (Hdc in next 5 hdc, 2 hdc in next hdc) around: 63 hdc.

Rnd 8: (Hdc in next 6 hdc, 2 hdc in next hdc) around: 72 hdc.

Rnd 9: (Hdc in next 7 hdc, 2 hdc in next hdc) around: 81 hdc.

Rnd 10: (Hdc in next 8 hdc, 2 hdc in next hdc) around: 90 hdc.

Rnd 11: (Hdc in next 9 hdc, 2 hdc in next hdc) around: 99 hdc.

Rnd 12: (Hdc in next 10 hdc, 2 hdc in next hdc) around: 108 hdc.

Rnds 13-25: Hdc in each hdc around.

Rnd 26: (Hdc in next 10 hdc, hdc2tog) around: 99 hdc.

Rnd 27: (Hdc in next 9 hdc, hdc2tog) around: 90 hdc.

Rnd 28: (Hdc in next 8 hdc, hdc2tog) around: 81 hdc.

Rnd 29: (Hdc in next 7 hdc, hdc2tog) around: 72 hdc.

Rnd 30: (Hdc in next 6 hdc, hdc2tog) around: 63 hdc.

Rnd 31: (Hdc in next 5 hdc, hdc2tog) around: 54 hdc.

Rnd 32: (Hdc in next 4 hdc, hdc2tog) around: 45 hdc.

Rnd 33: (Hdc in next 3 hdc, hdc2tog) around: 36 hdc.

Rnd 34: (Hdc in next 2 hdc, hdc2tog) around: 27 hdc.

Rnd 35: (Hdc in next hdc, hdc2tog) around: 18 hdc.

Stuff firmly.

Rnd 36: Hdc2tog 9 times: 9 hdc.

Rnd 37: Hdc in next 9 hdc; slip st in next hdc, finish off leaving a long end for sewing.

Thread yarn needle with long end and weave needle through sts on Rnd 37 ***(Fig. 7, page 78)***.

Rascal Raccoon

EASY+

FINISHED SIZE

16" (40.5 cm) tall

GAUGE INFORMATION

16 sc and 16 rows/rnds = 4" (10 cm)

Gauge Swatch:
4" (10 cm) square

Ch 17.

Row 1: Sc in second ch from hook and in each ch across: 16 sc.

Rows 2-16: Ch 1, turn; sc in each sc across.

Finish off.

SHOPPING LIST

Yarn (Medium Weight) 4

[3.5 ounces, 170 yards (100 grams 156 meters) per skein**]**:

- ☐ Gray - 2 skeins
- ☐ White - 1 skein
- ☐ Black - 1 skein

Crochet Hook

- ☐ Size F (3.75 mm) **or** size needed for gauge

Additional Supplies

- ☐ Yarn needle
- ☐ Safety pin
- ☐ Sewing pins
- ☐ 12 mm safety eyes - 2
- ☐ Polyester fiberfill

STITCH GUIDE

SINGLE CROCHET 2 TOGETHER *(abbreviated sc2tog)*

Pull up a loop in each of next 2 sts, YO and draw through all 3 loops on hook **(counts as one sc)**.

DOUBLE CROCHET 2 TOGETHER *(abbreviated dc2tog)*

★ YO, insert hook in **next** st, YO and pull up a loop, YO and draw through 2 loops on hook; repeat from ★ once **more**, YO and draw through all 3 loops on hook **(counts as one dc)**.

ARM *(Make 2)*

Stuff Arm firmly while working.

Rnd 1 (Right side)**:** With Black, ch 2, 5 sc in second ch from hook; do **not** join, place marker to indicate beginning of rnd ***(see Markers, page 77)***.

Note: Loop a short piece of yarn around any stitch to mark Rnd 1 as **right** side.

Rnd 2: 2 Sc in each sc around: 10 sc

Rnd 3: (Sc in next sc, 2 sc in next sc) around: 15 sc.

Rnds 4 and 5: Sc in each sc around.

Rnd 6: (Sc in next 3 sc, sc2tog) around: 12 sc.

Rnd 7: (Sc in next 4 sc, sc2tog) around: 10 sc.

Rnd 8: Sc in each sc around; slip st in next sc, finish off.

Rnd 9: With **right** side facing, skip next 3 sc from slip st on Rnd 8 and join Gray with sc in next sc ***(see Joining With Sc, page 77)***; sc in each sc around; join with slip st to first sc.

Rnd 10: Ch 1, sc in same st as joining and in each sc around; do **not** join, place marker to indicate beginning of rnd.

Rnds 11-26: Sc in each sc around.

Rnd 27: Sc in each sc around; slip st in next sc, finish off.

Stuff paws and lower Arms lightly, leaving top unstuffed.

LEG *(Make 2)*

Stuff Leg firmly while working.

With Black, ch 10.

Rnd 1 (Right side)**:** Sc in second ch from hook and in next 7 chs, 3 sc in last ch; working in free loops of beginning ch ***(Fig. 3b, page 77)***, sc in next 7 chs, 3 sc in last ch; join with slip st to first sc: 21 sc.

Note: Mark Rnd 1 as **right** side.

Rnd 2: Ch 1, sc in same st as joining and in next 7 sc, 3 sc in next sc, 2 sc in next sc, 3 sc in next sc, sc in next 7 sc, 2 sc in next 3 sc; join with slip st to first sc: 29 sc.

Rnd 3: Ch 1, sc in same st as joining and in next 7 sc, (sc in next sc, 2 sc in next sc) 4 times, sc in next 7 sc, (sc in next sc, 2 sc in next sc) 3 times; join with slip st to first sc: 36 sc.

Rnd 4: Ch 1, sc in same st as joining and in each sc around; join with slip st to first sc.

Rnd 5: Ch 1, sc in same st as joining and in next 6 sc, dc2tog 7 times, sc in last 15 sc; join with slip st to first sc: 29 sts.

Rnd 6: Ch 1, sc in same st as joining and in next 5 sc, dc2tog twice, dc in next st, dc2tog twice, sc in last 14 sc; join with slip st to first sc: 25 sts.

Rnd 7: Ch 1, sc in same st as joining and in next sc, dc2tog 3 times, dc in next st, dc2tog 3 times, sc in last 10 sc; join with slip st to first sc: 19 sts.

Rnd 8: Ch 1, sc in same st as joining and in next 2 sts, sc2tog, sc in next st, sc2tog, sc in each st around; join with slip st to first sc changing to Gray ***(Fig. 5b, page 77)***, cut Black: 17 sc.

Rnd 9: Ch 1, sc in same st as joining and in each sc around; join with slip st to first sc.

Rnd 10: Ch 1, sc in same st as joining and in each sc around; do **not** join, place marker to indicate beginning of rnd.

Rnds 11-13: Sc in each sc around.

Rnd 14: 2 Sc in next sc, sc in next 16 sc: 18 sc.

Rnd 15: Sc in each sc around.

Rnd 16: 2 Sc in next sc, sc in next 17 sc: 19 sc.

Rnds 17-19: Sc in each sc around.

Rnd 20: 2 Sc in next sc, sc in next 18 sc; finish off: 20 sc.

BODY

Rnd 1: With **right** sides facing, join Gray with sc in inside center of one Leg; ch 2, sc in inside center of second Leg, sc in each sc around second Leg and in next 2 chs; sc in each sc around first Leg; do **not** join, place marker to indicate beginning of rnd: 42 sc and 2 chs.

Rnd 2: 2 Sc in next sc, sc in free loops of next 2 chs, sc in next 19 sc, 2 sc in next sc, sc in next 21 sc: 46 sc.

Rnd 3: Sc in each sc around.

Rnd 4: Sc in next 25 sc, 2 sc in each of next 2 sc, sc in next 19 sc: 48 sc.

Rnds 5 and 6: Sc in each sc around.

Rnd 7: Sc in next 25 sc, (sc in next sc, 2 sc in next sc) twice, sc in next 19 sc: 50 sc.

Rnds 8-12: Sc in each sc around.

Rnd 13: Sc in next 15 sc, sc2tog, sc in next 23 sc, sc2tog, sc in next 8 sc: 48 sc.

Rnd 14: Sc in each sc around.

Rnd 15: (Sc in next 10 sc, sc2tog) around: 44 sc.

Rnds 16-18: Sc in each sc around.

Rnd 19: (Sc in next 9 sc, sc2tog) around: 40 sc.

Rnds 20 and 21: Sc in each sc around.

Rnd 22: (Sc in next 8 sc, sc2tog) around: 36 sc.

Rnds 23 and 24: Sc in each sc around.

Rnd 25: (Sc in next 10 sc, sc2tog) around: 33 sc.

Rnds 26 and 27: Sc in each sc around.

Rnd 28: Sc2tog, sc in next 31 sc: 32 sc.

Rnds 29 and 30: Sc in each sc around.

Rnd 31: Sc2tog, sc in next 30 sc: 31 sc.

Rnd 32: Sc in each sc around.

Rnd 33: Sc2tog, sc in next 29 sc: 30 sc.

Rnd 34: Sc in each sc around.

Place loop from hook onto safety pin to prevent Body from unraveling while pinning Arms to Body.

Flatten Rnd 27 of each Arm with slip st at fold. Pin Arms to Rnd 34, spacing 10 sc apart. Remove loop from safety pin and place loop onto hook.

Rnd 35 (Arm Joining)**:** Working through **all** layers, sc in each sc around.

Rnd 36: (Sc in next sc, sc2tog) around: 20 sc.

Stuff Body firmly.

Rnd 37: (Sc in next 2 sc, sc2tog) around; slip st in next sc: 15 sc.

Rnd 38: Ch 1, sc in same st as slip st and in each sc around; join with slip st to first sc.

Rnd 39: Ch 1, sc in same st as joining and in each sc around; join with slip st to first sc.

Rnd 40: Ch 1, working in Back Loops Only ***(Fig. 2, page 77)***, sc in each sc around; do **not** join, place marker to indicate beginning of rnd.

Rnds 41-44: Sc in both loops of each sc around.

Stuff Rnds 40-44 firmly.

Rnd 45: (Sc in next sc, sc2tog) around: 10 sc.

Rnd 46: Sc2tog 5 times; slip st in next sc, finish off: 5 sc.

HEAD

Rnd 1: With **right** side facing and working in free loops of sc on Rnd 39 ***(Fig. 3a, page 77)***, join Gray with sc in center sc at back neck; sc in same st, 2 sc in each of next 14 sc; join with slip st to first sc: 30 sc.

Rnd 2: Ch 1, (sc in next 4 sc, 2 sc in next sc) around; do **not** join, place marker to indicate beginning of rnd: 36 sc.

Rnd 3: (Sc in next 5 sc, 2 sc in next sc) around: 42 sc.

Rnd 4: (Sc in next 6 sc, 2 sc in next sc) around: 48 sc.

Rnd 5: (Sc in next 7 sc, 2 sc in next sc) around: 54 sc.

Rnds 6-15: Sc in each sc around.

Rnd 16: (Sc in next 7 sc, sc2tog) around: 48 sc.

Rnd 17: (Sc in next 6 sc, sc2tog) around: 42 sc.

Rnd 18: (Sc in next 5 sc, sc2tog) around: 36 sc.

Rnd 19: (Sc in next 4 sc, sc2tog) around: 30 sc.

Rnd 20: (Sc in next 3 sc, sc2tog) around: 24 sts.

Rnd 21: (Sc in next 2 sc, sc2tog) around: 18 sc.

Stuff Head firmly.

Rnd 22: (Sc in next sc, sc2tog) around: 12 sc.

Rnd 23: Sc2tog 6 times; finish off leaving a long end for sewing: 6 sc.

Thread yarn needle with long end and weave needle through sts on Rnd 23 ***(Fig. 7, page 78)***; pull **tightly** to close and secure end.

EYE PATCH ***(Make 2)***
Rnd 1 (Right side)**:** With Black, ch 2, 6 sc in second ch from hook; join with slip st to first sc.

Note: Mark Rnd 1 as **right** side.

Rnd 2: Ch 1, 2 sc in each st around; join with slip st to first sc: 12 sc.

Rnd 3: Ch 1, sc in same st as joining and in next sc, 2 sc in next sc, sc in next sc, 2 sc in next sc, dc in next sc, (2 dc, ch 1, 2 dc) in next sc, dc in next sc, (sc in next sc, 2 sc in next sc) twice; join with slip st to first sc, finish off leaving a long end for sewing.

EYE ***(Make 2)***
Rnd 1 (Right side)**:** With White, ch 2, 5 sc in second ch from hook; join with slip st to first sc.

Note: Mark Rnd 1 as **right** side.

Rnd 2: Ch 1, 2 sc in each sc around; join with slip st to first sc, finish off leaving a long end for sewing.

Securely attach safety eyes to Eyes.

Sew Eye to Eye Patch.

Sew Eye Patches to Head.

MUZZLE
Rnd 1 (Right side)**:** With White, ch 2, 4 sc in second ch from hook; join with slip st to first sc.

Note: Mark Rnd 1 as **right** side.

Rnd 2: Ch 1, 2 sc in same st as joining and in each sc around; join with slip st to first sc: 8 sc.

Rnd 3: Ch 1, sc in same st as joining, 2 sc in next sc, (sc in next sc, 2 sc in next sc) around; join with slip st to first sc: 12 sc.

Rnd 4: Ch 1, sc in same st as joining and in next sc, 2 sc in next sc, (sc in next 2 sc, 2 sc in next sc) around; join with slip st to first sc: 16 sc.

Rnds 5 and 6: Ch 1, sc in each sc around; join with slip st to first sc.

Finish off leaving a long end for sewing.

With Black, add satin stitch nose and straight stitch mouth ***(see Embroidery Stitches, page 79)***.

Sew Muzzle to Head, stuffing **lightly** before closing.

EAR ***(Make 2)***
Rnd 1 (Right side)**:** With Black, ch 2, 4 sc in second ch from hook; join with slip st to first sc.

Note: Mark Rnd 1 as **right** side.

Rnd 2: Ch 1, 2 sc in same st as joining and in each sc around; join with slip st to first sc: 8 sc.

Rnd 3: Ch 1, sc in same st as joining and in each sc around; join with slip st to first sc changing to Gray, cut Black.

Rnd 4: Ch 1, sc in same st as joining, 2 sc in next sc, (sc in next sc, 2 sc in next sc) around; join with slip st to first sc: 12 sc.

Rnd 5: Ch 1, sc in each sc around; join with slip st to first sc, finish off leaving a long end for sewing.

Flatten Rnd 5 with yarn end at fold and sew Ears to Head.

TAIL

POM-POMS ***(Make 5 Total)***
With Black, make three 3" (7.5 cm) pom-poms ***(Figs. 10a-c, pages 78 and 79)*** and with Gray, make two.

Alternating colors and using long ends, join pom-poms together to form Tail.

Sew Tail to back of Body.

Rustic Throw

EASY

FINISHED SIZE

34" wide x 54" long
(86.5 cm x 137 cm)

GAUGE INFORMATION

In pattern, 9 sts and 7 rows = 4" (10 cm)

Gauge Swatch:
4" (10 cm)

Ch 10.

Rows 1-7: Work same as Throw on page 45: 9 linked dc.

Finish off.

SHOPPING LIST

Yarn (Bulky Weight) BULKY 5

[5 ounces, 132 yards
(141 grams, 121 meters) per skein**]**:

☐ 8 skeins

Crochet Hook

☐ Size M/N (9 mm)
or size needed for gauge

STITCH GUIDE

BEGINNING LINKED DOUBLE CROCHET

(abbreviated beginning linked dc)

Insert hook in second ch from hook, YO and pull up a loop, insert hook in first st, YO and pull up a loop (3 loops on hook), (YO and draw through 2 loops on hook) twice.

LINKED DOUBLE CROCHET

(abbreviated linked dc)

Insert hook in horizontal bar of previous linked dc ***(Fig. A)***, YO and pull up a loop, insert hook in next st, YO and pull up a loop (3 loops on hook) ***(Fig. B)***, (YO and draw through 2 loops on hook) twice ***(Fig. C)***.

Fig. A

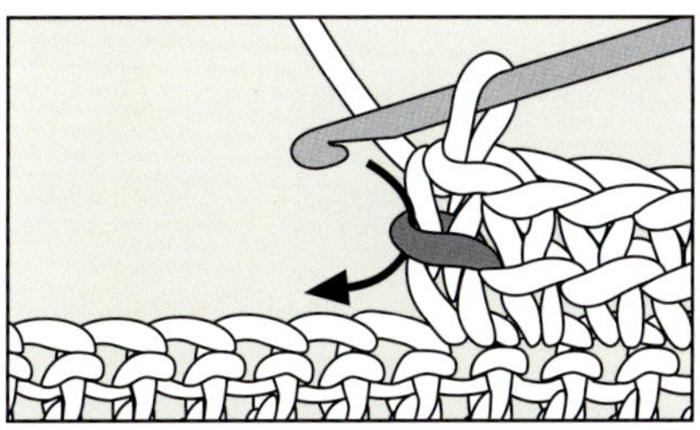

Fig. B

Fig. C

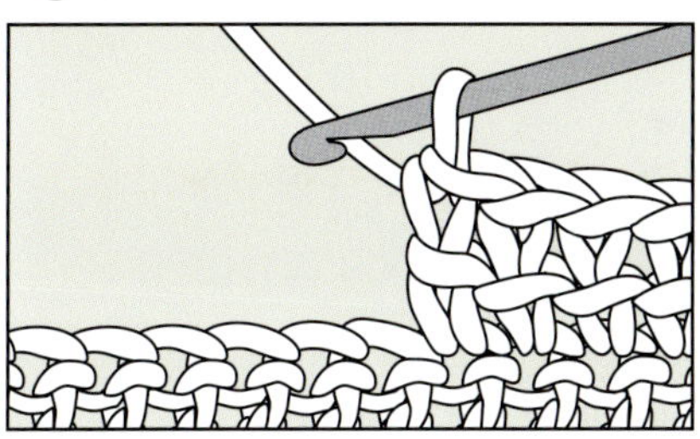

THROW

Ch 77.

Row 1 (Right side)**:** Sc in second ch from hook and in each ch across: 76 sc.

Note: Loop a short piece of yarn around any stitch to mark Row 1 as **right** side.

Row 2: Ch 2 **(does not count as a st, now and throughout)**, turn; working in Front Loops Only ***(Fig. 2, page 77)***, hdc in first sc and each sc across.

Row 3: Ch 3, turn; working in Back Loops Only, work beginning linked dc in first hdc, work linked dc in next hdc and in each hdc across.

Row 4: Ch 1, turn; sc in Front Loop Only of each linked dc across.

Row 5: Ch 3, turn; working in Back Loops Only, work beginning linked dc in first sc, work linked dc in each sc across.

Row 6: Ch 2, turn; hdc in Front Loop Only of each sc across.

Row 7: Repeat Row 3.

Row 8: Ch 1, turn; sc in Back Loop Only of each linked dc across.

Rows 9-70: Repeat Rows 2-8, 8 times; then repeat Rows 2-7 once **more**, do **not** finish off.

TRIM

Rnd 1: Ch 3, do **not** turn; work linked dc evenly across ends of rows; working in free loops of beginning ch ***(Fig. 3b, page 77)***, work 3 linked dc in first ch, work linked dc in each ch across to last ch, work 3 linked dc in last ch; work linked dc evenly across ends of rows; work 3 linked dc in first st, work linked dc in each st across to last st, work 3 linked dc in last st; join with slip st to first linked dc.

Rnd 2: Ch 1, sc in Back Loop Only of each linked dc around working 3 sc in center linked dc of each corner; join with slip st to **both** loops of first sc, finish off.

Lamb Curtain Tie

EASY

FINISHED SIZE

6½" (16.5 cm) tall

GAUGE INFORMATION

20 sc and 20 rows = 4" (10 cm)

Gauge Swatch:
4" (10 cm) square

Ch 21.

Row 1: Sc in second ch from hook and in each ch across: 20 sc.

Rows 2-20: Ch 1, turn; sc in each sc across.

Finish off.

SHOPPING LIST

Yarn (Medium Weight) 4
[3.5 ounces, 210 yards (100 grams, 192 meters) per skein**]**:

- ☐ Off White - 1 skein
- ☐ Dark Gray - 1 skein
- ☐ Gray - 1 skein

Crochet Hook

- ☐ Size G (4 mm) **or** size needed for gauge

Additional Supplies

- ☐ Yarn needle
- ☐ 12 mm safety eyes - 2
- ☐ Polyester fiberfill

STITCH GUIDE

PUFF STITCH (uses one st)
★ YO twice, insert hook in st indicated, YO and pull up a loop, (YO and draw through 2 loops on hook) twice; repeat from ★ 2 times **more**, YO and draw through all 4 loops on hook.

SINGLE CROCHET 2 TOGETHER ***(abbreviated sc2tog)***
Pull up a loop in each of next 2 sc, YO and draw through all 3 loops on hook **(counts as one sc)**.

SINGLE CROCHET 3 TOGETHER ***(abbreviated sc3tog)***
Pull up a loop in each of next 3 sc, YO and draw through all 4 loops on hook **(counts as one sc)**.

BODY

With Off White, ch 32.

Row 1 (Right side)**:** Sc in second ch from hook and in each ch across: 31 sc.

Note: Loop a short piece of yarn around any stitch to mark Row 1 as **right** side.

Row 2: Ch 1, turn; sc in first sc, ★ work Puff St in next sc, sc in next sc; repeat from ★ across: 16 sc and 15 Puff Sts.

Row 3: Ch 1, turn; sc in each st across: 31 sc.

Row 4: Ch 1, turn; sc in first 2 sc, work Puff St in next sc, ★ sc in next sc, work Puff St in next sc; repeat from ★ across to last 2 sc, sc in last 2 sc: 17 sc and 14 Puff Sts.

Row 5: Ch 1, turn; sc in each st across: 31 sc.

Row 6: Repeat Row 2: 16 sc and 14 Puff Sts.

Row 7: Ch 1, turn; sc in each st across.

Row 8 (Decrease row)**:** Ch 1, turn; sc2tog, work Puff St in next sc, ★ sc in next sc, work Puff St in next sc; repeat from ★ across to last 2 sc, sc2tog: 29 sts.

Rows 9-14: Repeat Rows 7 and 8, 3 times: 23 sts.

Row 15: Ch 1, turn; sc in each st across.

Row 16: Ch 1, turn; sc3tog, sc in next sc, ★ work Puff St in next sc, sc in next sc; repeat from ★ across to last 3 sc, sc3tog; finish off leaving a long end for sewing: 19 sts.

With **wrong** side facing, sew ends of rows together; do **not** cut yarn. Turn **right** side out.

Weave yarn through sts on Row 1 ***(Fig. 7, page 78)*** and pull **tightly** to close; secure end.

Stuff Body firmly.

HEAD

Rnd 1 (Right side)**:** With Gray, ch 2, 6 sc in second ch from hook; do **not** join, place marker to indicate beginning of rnd ***(see Markers, page 77)***.

Note: Mark Rnd 1 as **right** side.

Rnd 2: 2 Sc in each sc around: 12 sc.

Rnd 3: Sc in each sc around.

Rnd 4: (Sc in next sc, 2 sc in next sc) around: 18 sc.

Rnd 5: Sc in each sc around.

Rnd 6: (Sc in next 2 sc, 2 sc in next sc) around: 24 sc.

Rnd 7: Sc in each sc around.

Rnd 8: (Sc in next 3 sc, 2 sc in next sc) around: 30 sc.

Rnd 9: Sc in each sc around.

Rnd 10: (Sc in next 4 sc, 2 sc in next sc) around: 36 sc.

Rnds 11 and 12: Sc in each sc around.

Rnd 13: Sc in each sc around; slip st in next sc, finish off.

Rnd 14: With **right** side facing, join Off White with sc in any sc ***(see Joining With Sc, page 77)***; sc in each sc around; join with slip st to first sc.

Rnd 15: Ch 1, **turn**; sc in same st as joining, work Puff St in next sc, ★ sc in next sc, work Puff St in next sc; repeat from ★ around; join with slip st to first sc.

Rnd 16: Ch 1, turn; sc in same st as joining and in each st around; join with slip st to first sc.

Rnd 17: Ch 2 **(does not count as a st)**, turn; work Puff St in same st as joining, sc in next sc, ★ work Puff St in next sc, sc in next sc; repeat from ★ around; join with slip st to first Puff St.

Rnd 18: Ch 1, turn; sc in same st as joining and in each st around; join with slip st to first sc.

Rnds 19-23: Repeat Rnds 15-18 once, then repeat Rnd 15 once **more**.

Finish off leaving a long end for sewing.

Attach safety eyes between Rnds 9 and 10 spaced 6 sc apart.

With Dark Gray and using straight stitch ***(see Embroidery Stitches, page 79)***, add nose to Head.

Stuff Head firmly.

Use yarn needle to weave through sts on Rnd 23 and pull **tightly** to close.

EAR *(Make 2)*

Rnd 1 (Right side)**:** With Gray, ch 2, 4 sc in second ch from hook, do **not** join; place marker to indicate beginning of rnd.

Rnd 2: 2 Sc in each sc around: 8 sc.

Rnd 3: (Sc in next sc, 2 sc in next sc) around: 12 sc.

Rnd 4: (Sc in next 2 sc, 2 sc in next sc) around: 16 sc.

Rnd 5: (Sc in next 3 sc, 2 sc in next sc) around: 20 sc.

Rnds 6-13: Sc in each sc around.

Rnd 14: (Sc in next 2 sc, sc2tog) around: 15 sc.

Rnd 15: (Sc in next sc, sc2tog) around: 10 sc.

Rnds 16 and 17: Sc in each sc around.

Finish off leaving a long end for sewing.

Weave long end through sts on Rnd 17 to gather Ear, then sew Ear to side of Head.

LEG *(Make 2)*

Rnd 1 (Right side)**:** With Dark Gray, ch 2, 5 sc in second ch from hook; do **not** join, place marker to indicate beginning of rnd.

Note: Mark Rnd 1 as **right** side.

Rnd 2: 2 Sc in each sc around: 10 sc.

Rnd 3: (Sc in next sc, 2 sc in next sc) around: 15 sc.

Rnd 4: (Sc in next 2 sc, 2 sc in next sc) around: 20 sc.

Rnds 5-7: Sc in each sc around.

Rnd 8: (Sc2tog, sc in next 2 sc) around: 15 sc.

Rnd 9: (Sc2tog, sc in next sc) around; slip st in next sc, finish off: 10 sc.

Rnd 10: With **right** side facing, skip slip st and next 3 sc, join Gray with sc in next sc; sc in each st around; join with slip st to first sc.

Rnd 11: Ch 1, sc in each sc around; do **not** join, place marker to indicate beginning of rnd.

Stuff Rnds 1-11 of Leg.

Rnds 12-19: Sc in each sc around.

Rnd 20: Sc in each sc around; slip st in next sc, finish off leaving a long end for sewing.

ARM *(Make 2)*

Rnds 1-11: Work same as Leg: 10 sc.

Stuff Rnds 1-11 of Arm.

Rnds 12-42: Sc in each sc around.

Rnd 43: Sc in each sc around; slip st in next sc; finish off leaving a long end for sewing.

FINISHING

Using photo as a guide, sew Head, Arms and Legs to Body.

Lamb Wall Hanging

EASY

FINISHED SIZE

9" wide x 13½" long
(23 cm x 34.5 cm)
excluding fringe and hanger

GAUGE INFORMATION

16 sc and 16 rows = 4" (10 cm)

Gauge Swatch:
4" (10 cm) square

Ch 17.

Row 1: Sc in second ch from hook and in each ch across: 16 sc.

Rows 2-16: Ch 1, turn; sc in each sc across.

Finish off.

SHOPPING LIST

Yarn (Medium Weight) MEDIUM 4
[3.5 ounces, 210 yards
(100 grams, 192 meters) per skein**]**:

- ☐ Off White - 1 skein
- ☐ Green - 1 skein
- ☐ Gray - 1 skein

Crochet Hook

- ☐ Size H (5 mm)
  or size needed for gauge

Additional Supplies

- ☐ Yarn needle
- ☐ 12" (30.5 cm) dowel rod

STITCH GUIDE

SINGLE CROCHET 2 TOGETHER *(abbreviated sc2tog)*

Pull up a loop in each of next 2 sc, YO and draw through all 3 loops on hook **(counts as one sc)**.

PANEL

With Off White, ch 35.

Row 1: Sc in back ridge of second ch from hook and in each ch across ***(Fig. 1, page 77)***: 34 sc.

Row 2 (Right side)**:** Ch 2 **(does not count as a st)**, turn; hdc in first sc and in each sc across.

Note: Loop a short piece of yarn around any stitch to mark Row 2 as **right** side.

Row 3: Ch 4, turn; skip first hdc, 2 sc in next hdc, (skip next hdc, 2 sc in next hdc) across: 34 sc and one ch-4.

Rows 4-52: Ch 4, turn; skip first sc, 2 sc in next sc, (skip next sc, 2 sc in next sc) across.

Rows 53-58: Ch 1, turn; sc in each sc across.

Finish off leaving a long end for sewing.

Sew top of Row 58 to **wrong** side of Row 52 to form a casing.

LAMB

With Green, ch 8.

Row 1 (Right side)**:** 2 Sc in second ch from hook, sc in next 5 chs, 2 sc in last ch: 9 sc.

Note: Mark Row 1 as **right** side.

Row 2: Ch 1, turn; working in Front Loops Only ***(Fig. 2, page 77)***, 2 sc in first sc, sc in next 7 sc, 2 sc in last sc: 11 sc.

Row 3 (Increase row)**:** Ch 1, turn; working in Back Loops Only, 2 sc in first sc, sc in each sc across to last sc, 2 sc in last sc: 13 sc.

Row 4 (Increase row)**:** Ch 1, turn; working in Front Loops Only, 2 sc in first sc, sc in each sc across to last sc, 2 sc in last sc: 15 sc.

Rows 5 and 6: Repeat Rows 3 and 4: 19 sc.

Row 7: Ch 1, turn; sc in Back Loop Only of each sc across.

Row 8: Repeat Row 4: 21 sc.

Row 9: Ch 1, turn; sc in Back Loop Only of each sc across.

Row 10: Repeat Row 4: 23 sc.

Row 11: Ch 1, turn; sc in Back Loop Only of each sc across.

Row 12: Ch 1, turn; sc in Front Loop Only of each sc across.

Row 13 (Decrease row)**:** Ch 1, turn; working in Back Loops Only, sc2tog, sc in each sc across to last 2 sc, sc2tog: 21 sc.

Row 14: Ch 1, turn; working in Front Loops Only, sc2tog twice, sc in next 13 sc, sc2tog twice: 17 sc.

Row 15: Repeat Row 13: 15 sc.

Row 16: Ch 1, turn; working in Front Loops Only, sc2tog, sc in each sc across to last 2 sc, sc2tog: 13 sc.

Row 17: Repeat Row 13: 11 sc.

Row 18: Repeat Row 4: 13 sc.

Row 19: Repeat Row 3: 15 sc.

Row 20: Ch 1, turn; sc in Front Loop Only of each sc across.

Row 21: Repeat Row 3: 17 sc.

Row 22: Ch 1, turn; sc in Front Loop Only of each sc across.

Row 23: Ch 1, turn; sc in Back Loop Only of each sc across.

Rows 24 and 25: Repeat Rows 22 and 23.

Row 26: Ch 1, turn; working in Front Loops Only, sc2tog, sc in next 13 sc, sc2tog: 15 sc.

Row 27: Ch 1, turn; working in Back Loops Only, sc2tog, sc in next 11 sc, sc2tog: 13 sc.

Row 28: Ch 1, turn; working in Front Loops Only, sc2tog, sc in next 9 sc, sc2tog: 11 sc.

Row 29: Ch 1, turn; sc in Back Loop Only of each sc across.

Row 30: Ch 1, turn; working in Front Loops Only, sc2tog, sc in next 7 sc, sc2tog: 9 sc.

Row 31: Ch 1, turn; working in Back Loops Only, sc2tog twice, sc in next sc, sc2tog twice: 5 sc.

Trim: Ch 1, do **not** turn; sc evenly around entire piece ***(Fig. 3b, page 77)***; join with slip st to first sc, finish off.

FACE

Row 1: With Off White, ch 3, 2 sc in second ch from hook and in last ch: 4 sc.

Row 2: Ch 1, turn; sc in each sc across.

Row 3: Ch 1, turn; 2 sc in first sc, sc in next 2 sc, 2 sc in last sc: 6 sc.

Row 4: Ch 1, turn; sc in each sc across.

Row 5: Ch 1, turn; 2 sc in first sc, sc in next 4 sc, 2 sc in last sc: 8 sc.

Row 6: Ch 1, turn; sc in each sc across.

Row 7: Ch 1, turn; 2 sc in first sc, sc in next 6 sc, 2 sc in last sc: 10 sc.

Row 8: Ch 1, turn; sc in each sc across.

Row 9: Ch 1, turn; 2 sc in first sc, sc in next 8 sc, 2 sc in last sc: 12 sc.

Row 10: Ch 1, turn; sc in each sc across.

Trim: Ch 1, do **not** turn; sc evenly across ends of rows; working in free loops of beginning ch, sc in each ch across; sc evenly across ends of rows, slip st in first sc of Row 10, finish off leaving a long end for sewing.

With Gray, add eyes, nose and mouth to Face ***(see Embroidery Stitches, page 79)***.

With **right** sides facing, sew Face to Body.

With **right** sides facing, sew Body to Panel.

WOOL

Working in free loops of sts on Body ***(Fig. 3a, page 77)***, begin at bottom (Row 1), and join Green with slip st in first sc; ★ working from **right** to **left**, (ch 4, slip st in next sc) across row; ch 4, slip st in sc on row above, rotate work; repeat from ★ across Body including partial rows around Face and Head. Finish off when all sts have been worked.

EAR *(Make 2)*

Row 1 (Right side)**:** With Gray, ch 2, 2 sc in second ch from hook.

Note: Mark Row 1 as **right** side.

Row 2: Ch 1, turn; 2 sc in each sc across: 4 sc.

Row 3: Ch 1, turn; 2 sc in first sc, sc in next 2 sc, 2 sc in last sc: 6 sc.

Rows 4-6: Ch 1, turn; sc in each sc across.

Row 7: Ch 1, turn; sc2tog, sc in next 2 sc, sc2tog: 4 sc.

Row 8: Ch 1, turn; sc2tog twice: 2 sc.

Trim: Ch 1, do **not** turn; sc evenly across ends of rows; (sc, ch 1, sc) in ch at tip of Ear; sc evenly across ends of rows to last row, slip st in last row; finish off.

LEG *(Make 2)*

With Gray, ch 4.

Row 1: Sc in second ch from hook and in each ch across: 3 sc.

Rows 2-4: Ch 1, turn; sc in each sc across.

Finish off leaving a long end for sewing.

FINISHING

With **right** sides facing, sew Ears and Legs to Body.

Slide dowel rod into casing.

Tie each end of a 18" (45.5 cm) strand of Cream on opposite ends of dowel rod. Hide ends within casing.

Holding 7 strands of yarn together, each 12" (30.5 cm) long, add fringe to bottom edge of Panel ***(Figs. 8a & b, page 78)***, using photo as a guide and alternating colors.

Swaddle Cocoon

EASY

FINISHED SIZE

Cocoon: 10" (25.5 cm) deep

Swaddling Wrap: 6" high x 43" wide (15 cm x 109 cm)

GAUGE INFORMATION

12 sc and 12 rows/rnds = 4" (10 cm)

Gauge Swatch:
4" (10 cm) square

Ch 13.

Row 1: Sc in second ch from hook and in each ch across: 12 sc.

Rows 2-12: Ch 1, turn; sc in each sc across.

Finish off.

SHOPPING LIST

Yarn (Bulky Weight) BULKY 5

[5 ounces, 132 yards (141 grams, 121 meters) per skein**]**:

☐ 3 skeins

Crochet Hook

☐ Size K (6.5 mm) **or** size needed for gauge

COCOON

Rnd 1 (Right side)**:** Ch 2, 8 sc in second ch from hook; do **not** join, place marker to indicate beginning of rnd ***(see Markers, page 77)***.

Note: Loop a short piece of yarn around any stitch to mark Rnd 1 as **right** side.

Rnd 2: 2 Sc in each sc around: 16 sc.

Rnd 3: (Sc in next sc, 2 sc in next sc) around: 24 sc.

Rnd 4: (Sc in next 2 sc, 2 sc in next sc) around: 32 sc.

Rnd 5: (Sc in next 3 sc, 2 sc in next sc) around: 40 sc.

Rnd 6: (Sc in next 4 sc, 2 sc in next sc) around: 48 sc.

Rnd 7: (Sc in next 5 sc, 2 sc in next sc) around: 56 sc.

Rnd 8: (Sc in next 6 sc, 2 sc in next sc) around: 64 sc.

Rnds 9-29: Sc in each sc around.

Rnd 30: Sc in each sc around; slip st in next sc, finish off.

SWADDLING WRAP

Row 1: Ch 40; with **right** side of Cocoon facing, skip slip st on Rnd 30 and sc in next 33 sc, leave remaining 31 sc unworked: 33 sc and 40 chs.

Row 2: Ch 42, turn; working in back ridge of chs ***(Fig. 1, page 77)***, dc in fourth ch from hook and in each ch and each sc across: 113 sts.

Row 3: Ch 3 **(counts as first dc, now and throughout)**, turn; ★ skip next dc, (dc, ch 1, dc) in next dc, skip next dc, dc in next st; repeat from ★ across: 85 dc and 28 chs.

Row 4: Ch 3, turn; dc in next dc and in each dc and each ch across: 113 dc.

Rows 5-10: Repeat Rows 3 and 4, 3 times.

Finish off.

Bunny Toy

EASY

FINISHED SIZE

5½" tall x 5" wide
(14 cm x 12.5 cm)
excluding ears and arms

GAUGE INFORMATION

16 sc and 16 rows = 4" (10 cm)

Gauge Swatch:
4" (10 cm) square

Ch 17.

Row 1: Sc in second ch from hook and in each ch across: 16 sc.

Rows 2-16: Ch 1, turn; sc in each sc across.

Finish off.

SHOPPING LIST

Yarn (Medium Weight) MEDIUM 4

[7 ounces, 432 yards
(198 grams, 395 meters) per skein**]**:

- ☐ White - 80 yards (73 meters)
- ☐ Gray - 20 yards (18.5 meters)
- ☐ Pink - 20 yards (18.5 meters)
- ☐ Blue - 20 yards (18.5 meters)

Crochet Hook

- ☐ Size G (4 mm)
  or size needed for gauge

Additional Supplies

- ☐ Yarn needle
- ☐ Sewing pins
- ☐ Polyester fiberfill

BODY *(Make 2)*

With White, ch 4.

Row 1 (Right side)**:** 2 Sc in second ch from hook, sc in next ch, 2 sc in last ch: 5 sc.

Note: Loop a short piece of yarn around any stitch to mark Row 1 as **right** side.

Row 2: Ch 1, turn; 2 sc in first sc, sc in next 3 sc, 2 sc in last sc: 7 sc.

Row 3: Ch 1, turn; 2 sc in first sc, sc in next 5 sc, 2 sc in last sc: 9 sc.

Row 4: Ch 1, turn; 2 sc in first sc, sc in next 7 sc, 2 sc in last sc: 11 sc.

Row 5: Ch 1, turn; 2 sc in first sc, sc in next 9 sc, 2 sc in last sc: 13 sc.

Row 6: Ch 1, turn; 2 sc in first sc, sc in next 11 sc, 2 sc in last sc: 15 sc.

Rows 7-11: Ch 1, turn; sc in each sc across.

Row 12: Ch 1, turn; sc in each sc across changing to Gray in last sc ***(Fig. 3a, page 77)***, drop White.

Row 13: Ch 1, turn; sc in each sc across.

Row 14: Ch 1, turn; sc in each sc across changing to White in last sc, cut Gray.

Row 15: Ch 1, turn; sc in each sc across.

Row 16: Ch 1, turn; sc in each sc across changing to Pink in last sc, drop White.

Row 17: Ch 1, turn; sc in each sc across.

Row 18: Ch 1, turn; sc in each sc across changing to White in last sc, cut Pink.

Row 19: Ch 1, turn; sc in each sc across.

Row 20: Ch 1, turn; sc in each sc across changing to Blue in last sc, drop White.

Row 21: Ch 1, turn; 2 sc in first sc, sc in next 13 sc, 2 sc in last sc: 17 sc.

Row 22: Ch 1, turn; sc in each sc across changing to White in last sc, cut Blue.

Trim: Ch 1, turn; 2 sc in first sc, sc in next 15 sc, 2 sc in last sc; sc evenly across ends of rows; working in free loops of beginning ch ***(Fig. 3b, page 77)***, sc in next 3 chs; sc evenly across ends of rows; join with slip st to first sc, finish off.

With **right** side facing and using photo as a guide, add Gray French knot eyes ***(see Embroidery Stitches, page 79)*** to one Body.

Using straight stitch, add Pink nose and Gray mouth.

FIRST EAR

Rnd 1 (Right side)**:** With White, ch 2, 4 sc in second ch from hook; join with slip st to first sc changing to Gray ***(Fig. 5b, page 77)***, cut White.

Note: Mark Rnd 1 as **right** side.

Rnd 2: Ch 1, 2 sc in same st as joining and in each sc around; join with slip st to first sc changing to Pink, cut Gray: 8 sc.

Rnd 3: Ch 1, sc in same st as joining, 2 sc in next sc, (sc in next sc, 2 sc in next sc) around; join with slip st to first sc changing to Blue, cut Pink: 12 sc.

Rnd 4: Ch 1, sc in same st as joining and in each sc around; join with slip st to first sc changing to White, cut Blue.

Rnds 5 and 6: Ch 1, sc in each sc around; join with slip st to first sc.

Rnd 7: Ch 1, sc in each sc around, do **not** join, place marker to indicate beginning of rnd ***(see Markers, page 77)***.

Rnds 8-13: Sc in each sc around.

Rnd 14: Sc in each sc around; slip st in next sc, finish off.

SECOND EAR

Rnd 1 (Right side)**:** With White, ch 2, 4 sc in second ch from hook; join with slip st to first sc.

Note: Mark Rnd 1 as **right** side.

Rnd 2: Ch 1, 2 sc in same st as joining and in each sc around; join with slip st to first sc: 8 sc.

Rnd 3: Ch 1, sc in same st as joining, 2 sc in next sc, (sc in next sc, 2 sc in next sc) around; join with slip st to first sc changing to Gray, drop White: 12 sc.

Rnd 4: Ch 1, sc in each sc around; join with slip st to first sc changing to White, cut Gray.

Rnd 5: Ch 1, sc in each sc around; join with slip st to first sc.

Rnd 6: Ch 1, sc in each sc around; join with slip st to first sc changing to Pink, drop White.

Rnd 7: Ch 1, sc in each sc around; join with slip st to first sc changing to White, cut Pink.

Rnd 8: Ch 1, sc in each sc around; join with slip st to first sc.

Rnd 9: Ch 1, sc in each sc around; join with slip st to first sc changing to Blue, drop White.

Rnd 10: Ch 1, sc in each sc around; join with slip st to first sc changing to White, cut Blue.

Rnds 11-14: Ch 1, sc in each sc around; join with slip st to first sc.

Finish off.

ARM *(Make 2)*

With Blue, ch 3.

Row 1: 2 Sc in second ch from hook, 2 sc in last ch: 4 sc.

Rows 2-5: Ch 1, turn; sc in each sc across.

Finish off.

FINISHING

Using photo as a guide, pin Ears and Arms to **wrong** side of front Body.

With White and working through **all** layers, sew Body together, stuffing lightly with fiberfill before closing.

Deer Lovie

EASY

FINISHED SIZE

Lovie: 13" x 14½" (33 cm x 37 cm)

GAUGE INFORMATION

With larger size hook, 14 dc and 7 rows = 4" (10 cm)

Gauge Swatch:
4" (10 cm)

With larger size hook and Tan, ch 16.

Row 1: Dc in fourth ch from hook **(3 skipped chs count as first dc)** and in each ch across: 14 dc.

Rows 2-7: Ch 3 **(counts as first dc)**, turn; dc in next dc and in each dc across.

Finish off.

SHOPPING LIST

Yarn (Medium Weight)

[3.5 ounces, 175 yards (100 grams, 160 meters) per skein**]**:

- ☐ Tan - 1 skein
- ☐ Cream - 1 skein
- ☐ Brown - 20 yards (18.5 meters)

Crochet Hooks

- ☐ Size H (5 mm) **and**
- ☐ Size F (3.75 mm)
  or sizes needed for gauge

Additional Supplies

- ☐ Yarn needle
- ☐ Polyester fiberfill

STITCH GUIDE

SINGLE CROCHET 2 TOGETHER

(abbreviated sc2tog)

Pull up a loop in each of next 2 sc, YO and draw through all 3 loops on hook **(counts as one sc)**.

LOVIE

With larger size hook and Tan, ch 44; place marker in third ch from hook for st placement.

Row 1 (Right side)**:** Dc in fourth ch from hook **(3 skipped chs count as first dc)** and in each ch across: 42 dc.

Note: Loop a short piece of yarn around any stitch to mark Row 1 as **right** side.

Row 2: Ch 3 **(counts as first dc)**, turn; dc in next dc, ★ ch 2, skip next 2 dc, dc in next 2 dc; repeat from ★ across: 22 dc and 10 ch-2 sps.

Row 3: Ch 3 **(counts as first dc)**, turn; dc in next dc, (2 dc in next ch-2 sp, dc in next 2 dc) across: 42 dc.

Rows 4-23: Repeat Rows 2 and 3, 10 times; do **not** finish off.

BORDER

Rnd 1: Ch 1, do **not** turn; sc evenly across ends of rows; working in free loops of beginning ch ***(Fig. 3b, page 77)***, 3 sc in first ch, sc in each ch across to marked ch, 3 sc in marked ch, remove marker; sc evenly across ends of rows to Row 23, 3 sc in first dc, sc in each dc across to last dc, 3 sc in last dc; join with slip st to first sc changing to Cream ***(Fig. 5b, page 77)***, cut Tan.

Rnd 2: Ch 1, sc in same st as joining and in each sc around working 3 sc in each corner sc; join with slip st to first sc changing to Brown, cut Cream.

Rnd 3: Ch 1, sc in same st as joining and in each sc around working 3 sc in each corner sc; join with slip st to first sc, finish off.

HEAD

Rnd 1 (Right side)**:** With smaller size hook and Tan, ch 2, 8 sc in second ch from hook; do **not** join, place marker to indicate beginning of rnd ***(see Markers, page 77)***.

Note: Mark Rnd 1 as **right** side.

Rnd 2: 2 Sc in each sc around: 16 sc.

Rnd 3: (Sc in next sc, 2 sc in next sc) around: 24 sc.

Rnd 4: (Sc in next 2 sc, 2 sc in next sc) around: 32 sc.

Rnd 5: (Sc in next 3 sc, 2 sc in next sc) around: 40 sc.

Rnds 6-10: Sc in each sc around.

Rnd 11: (Sc in next 3 sc, sc2tog) around: 32 sc.

Rnd 12: Sc in each sc around.

Rnd 13: (Sc in next 2 sc, sc2tog) around: 24 sc.

Rnd 14: (Sc in next sc, sc2tog) around: 16 sc.

Rnds 15-17: Sc in each sc around.

Stuff Head with polyester fiberfill.

Rnd 18: Sc2tog around: 8 sc.

Rnd 19: Sc in each sc around; slip st in next sc, finish off leaving long end for sewing.

Weave long end through sts on Rnd 19 ***(Fig. 7, page 78)*** and pull **tightly** to close.

Using photo as a guide and Brown, add straight stitch eyes and satin stitch nose to Head ***(see Embroidery Stitches, page 79)***.

OUTER EAR *(Make 2)*

Row 1 (Right side)**:** With smaller size hook and Tan, ch 2, 2 sc in second ch from hook.

Note: Mark Row 1 as **right** side.

Row 2: Ch 1, turn; 2 sc in each sc across: 4 sc.

Row 3: Ch 1, turn; 2 sc in first sc, sc in next 2 sc, 2 sc in last sc: 6 sc.

Row 4: Ch 1, turn; 2 sc in first sc, sc in next 4 sc, 2 sc in last sc: 8 sc.

Rows 5-9: Ch 1, turn; sc in each sc across.

Row 10: Ch 1, turn; sc2tog, sc in next 4 sc, sc2tog: 6 sc.

Row 11: Ch 1, turn; sc2tog, sc in next 2 sc, sc2tog; finish off: 4 sc.

INNER EAR *(Make 2)*

With Cream, work same as Outer Ear.

EAR JOINING

With **wrong** sides of one Inner Ear and one Outer Ear together, with Inner Ear facing and working in ends of rows through **both** layers, join Tan with sc in Row 11 ***(see Joining With Sc, page 77)***; sc evenly across to free loop of ch at tip, (sc, ch 1, sc) in ch, sc evenly across to opposite side; finish off leaving a long end for sewing.

Repeat for remaining Inner and Outer Ear.

SPOT *(Make 3)*

Rnd 1: With smaller size hook and Cream, ch 2, 6 sc in second ch from hook; join with slip st to first sc, finish off leaving a long end for sewing.

FINISHING

Using photo as guide for placement and long ends:

Sew Ears to Head.

Sew Head to center of Lovie.

Sew Spots to Lovie.

Owl Mobile

EASY

FINISHED SIZE

Each Owl: 4" (10 cm) high

GAUGE INFORMATION

10 sc and 10 rnds = 2" (5 cm)

Gauge Swatch:
2" (5 cm) diameter

Rnds 1-5: Work same as Body on page 66: 25 sc.

SHOPPING LIST

Yarn (Bulky Weight) 5

[3.5 ounces, 127 yards (100 grams, 116 meters) per set of 5 colors**]**:

- ☐ 1 set **[**approximately 25 yards (23 meters) per ball**]**
- ☐ Yellow scrap yarn - small amount for beaks

Crochet Hook

- ☐ Size F (3.75 mm) **or** size needed for gauge

Additional Supplies

- ☐ Yarn needle
- ☐ 12 mm safety eyes - 8
- ☐ Polyester fiberfill
- ☐ 14" (35.5 cm) grapevine wreath
- ☐ Cotton cording (for hanger)

STITCH GUIDE

TREBLE CROCHET

(abbreviated tr)

YO twice, insert hook in st indicated, YO and pull up a loop (4 loops on hook), (YO and draw through 2 loops on hook) 3 times.

SINGLE CROCHET 2 TOGETHER

(abbreviated sc2tog)

Pull up a loop in each of next 2 sc, YO and draw through all 3 loops on hook **(counts as one sc)**.

BODY

(Make one each with 4 darkest colors of yarn set)

Rnd 1 (Right side)**:** Ch 2, 5 sc in second ch from hook; do **not** join, place marker to indicate beginning of rnd ***(see Markers, page 77)***.

Note: Loop a short piece of yarn around any stitch to mark Rnd 1 as **right** side.

Rnd 2: 2 Sc in each sc around: 10 sc.

Rnd 3: (Sc in next sc, 2 sc in next sc) around: 15 sc.

Rnd 4: (Sc in next 2 sc, 2 sc in next sc) around: 20 sc.

Rnd 5: (Sc in next 3 sc, 2 sc in next sc) around: 25 sc.

Rnd 6: (Sc in next 4 sc, 2 sc in next sc) around: 30 sc.

Rnd 7: (Sc in next 5 sc, 2 sc in next sc) around: 35 sc.

Rnds 8-11: Sc in each sc around.

Rnd 12: (Sc2tog, sc in next 5 sc) around: 30 sc.

Rnd 13: (Sc2tog, sc in next 4 sc) around: 25 sc.

Rnd 14: Sc in each sc around.

Rnd 15: (Sc2tog, sc in next 3 sc) around: 20 sc.

Rnds 16-18: Sc in each sc around.

Rnd 19: (Sc2tog, sc in next 2 sc) around: 15 sc.

Rnd 20: (Sc2tog, sc in next sc) around: 10 sc.

Stuff Body with polyester fiberfill.

Row 1 (Joining row)**:** Fold last rnd with yarn at side; working through **both** layers, sc in each sc across: 5 sc.

Row 2: Turn; (ch 5, slip st, ch 6, slip st) in first sc, ch 5, slip st in next 3 sc, (ch 5, slip st, ch 6, slip st, ch 5, slip st) in last sc; finish off.

EYE *(Make 2)*

Rnd 1: With lightest color, ch 4, 9 dc in fourth ch from hook; join with slip st to top of beginning ch, finish off leaving a long end for sewing.

Add safety eye to center of Eye.

Sew Eyes to front.

With Yellow and using straight st ***(see Embroidery Stitches, page 79)***, add beak.

WING *(Make 2)*

With lightest color, ch 9.

Rnd 1: Sc in second ch from hook, hdc in next ch, dc in next ch, tr in next 3 chs, dc in next ch, 5 hdc in last ch; working in free loops of beginning ch ***(Fig. 3b, page 77)***, dc in next ch, tr in next 3 chs, dc in next ch, hdc in next ch, slip st in next ch; join with slip st to first sc, finish off leaving long end for sewing.

Using photo as a guide, sew one Wing to **each** side of Body.

ASSEMBLY

Cut 4 strands of cotton cording, each 28" (71 cm) long. Holding all 4 strands together, make an 1" (2.5 cm) slip knot approximately 4" (10 cm) from ends, wrap knot with long ends to hide knot and secure ends. Attach free end of each strand with a knot to wreath, evenly spaced around. Pull free ends through wreath and adjust knots to make sure that wreath will hang level. Trim cording to approximately 7" (18 cm) from wreath and tie a knot to Row 2 on top of each Owl. Pull end of cording into Body to hide.

Woodland Rug

EASY

FINISHED SIZE

25" wide x 38" long
(63.5 cm x 96.5 cm)

GAUGE INFORMATION

14 dc and 8 rows = 4" (10 cm)

Gauge Swatch:
4" (10 cm) square

Ch 16.

Row 1: Dc in fourth ch from hook **(3 skipped chs count as first dc)** and in each ch across: 14 dc.

Rows 2-8: Ch 3 **(counts as first dc)**, turn; dc in next dc and in each dc across.

Finish off.

SHOPPING LIST

Yarn (Medium Weight) MEDIUM 4

[3 ounces, 197 yards
(85 grams, 180 meters) per skein**]**:

- ☐ Brown - 3 skeins
- ☐ Gray - 1 skein
- ☐ Cream - 1 skein

Crochet Hook

- ☐ Size I (5.5 mm)
  or size needed for gauge

RUG

With Gray, ch 81.

Row 1 (Right side)**:** Sc in second ch from hook and in each across: 80 sc.

Note: Loop a short piece of yarn around any stitch to mark Row 1 as **right** side.

Row 2: Ch 1, turn; sc in each sc across changing to Brown in last sc ***(Fig. 5a, page 77)***, cut Gray.

Rows 3-8: Ch 3 **(counts as first dc, now and throughout)**, turn; dc in next st and in each st across; at end of Row 8, change to Gray in last dc, cut Brown.

Row 9: Ch 3, turn; dc in next dc and in each dc across changing to Brown in last dc, cut Gray.

Row 10: Ch 3, turn; dc in next st and in each st across changing to Cream in last dc, cut Brown.

Row 11: Ch 1, turn; sc in each dc across changing to Brown in last sc, cut Cream.

Rows 12-17: Repeat Rows 10 and 11, 3 times.

Row 18: Ch 3, turn; dc in next sc and in each sc across changing to Gray in last dc, cut Brown.

Row 19: Ch 3, turn; dc in next dc and in each dc across changing to Brown in last dc, cut Gray.

Rows 20-22: Ch 3, turn; dc in next dc and in each dc across; at end of Row 22, change to Gray in last dc, cut Brown.

Rows 23-33: Repeat Rows 9-19.

Rows 34-48: Ch 3, turn; dc in next dc and in each dc across; at end of Row 48, change to Gray in last dc, cut Brown.

Rows 49-73: Repeat Rows 9-33.

Rows 74-79: Ch 3, turn; dc in next dc and in each dc across; at end of Row 79, change to Gray in last dc, cut Brown.

Rows 80 and 81: Ch 1, turn; sc in each st across.

Do **not** finish off.

Edging: Ch 1, do **not** turn; sc evenly across ends of rows; working in free loops of beginning ch ***(Fig. 3b, page 77)***, 3 sc in first ch, sc in next 78 chs, 3 sc in next ch; sc evenly across ends of rows; 3 sc in first sc, sc in each sc across to last sc, 3 sc in last sc; join with slip st to first sc, finish off.

FRINGE

Holding 3 strands of Gray, each 10" (25.5 cm) long, add fringe in every fifth sc across each short edge ***(Figs. 8a & b, page 78)***.

Wipes Case

EASY

FINISHED SIZE

8½" high x 10" wide
(21.5 cm x 25.5 cm) opened

GAUGE INFORMATION

In pattern,
17 sts and 10 rows = 4" (10 cm)

Gauge Swatch:
4" (10 cm) square

Ch 19.

Row 1: Dc in fourth ch from hook **(3 skipped chs count as first dc)**and in each dc across: 17 dc.

Row 2: Ch 3 **(counts as first dc, now and throughout)**, turn; skip next dc, (dc, ch 1, dc) in next dc, ★ skip next 2 dc, (dc, ch 1, dc) in next dc; repeat from ★ across to last 2 dc, skip next dc, dc in last dc: 12 dc and 5 ch-1 sps.

Rows 3-10: Ch 3, turn; skip next dc, (dc, ch 1, dc) in next ch-1 sp, ★ skip next 2 dc, (dc, ch 1, dc) in next ch-1 sp; repeat from ★ across to last 2 dc, skip next dc, dc in last dc.

Finish off.

SHOPPING LIST

Yarn (Medium Weight) 4

[3.5 ounces, 246 yards
(100 grams, 225 meters) per skein**]**:

☐ Blue - 1 skein

[3.5 ounces, 170 yards
(100 grams, 156 meters) per skein**]**:

☐ White - 1 skein

Crochet Hook

☐ Size F (3.75 mm)
or size needed for gauge

Additional Supplies

☐ Yarn needle

STITCH GUIDE

BACK POST DOUBLE CROCHET *(abbreviated BPdc)*

YO, insert hook from **back** to **front** around post of st indicated ***(Fig. 4, page 77)***, YO and pull up a loop (3 loops on hook), (YO and draw through 2 loops on hook) twice.

FRONT POST TREBLE CROCHET *(abbreviated FPtr)*

YO twice, insert hook from **front** to **back** around post of st indicated ***(Fig. 4, page 77)***, YO and pull up a loop (4 loops on hook), (YO and draw through 2 loops on hook) 3 times.

BACK POST TREBLE CROCHET *(abbreviated BPtr)*

YO twice, insert hook from **back** to **front** around post of st indicated ***(Fig. 4, page 77)***, YO and pull up a loop (4 loops on hook), (YO and draw through 2 loops on hook) 3 times.

BODY

With Blue, ch 87, place marker in third ch from hook for st placement.

Row 1: Dc in fourth ch from hook **(3 skipped chs count as first dc)** and in each ch across: 85 dc.

Row 2 (Right side)**:** Ch 3 **(counts as first dc, now and throughout)**, turn; dc in next dc, skip next dc, (dc, ch 1, dc) in next dc, skip next dc, work FPtr around each of next 3 dc, skip next dc, (dc, ch 1, dc) in next dc, ★ skip next 2 dc, (dc, ch 1, dc) in next dc; repeat from ★ across to last 9 dc, skip next dc, work FPtr around each of next 3 dc, skip next dc, (dc, ch 1, dc) in next dc, skip next dc, dc in last 2 dc: 60 sts and 25 ch-1 sps.

Note: Loop a short piece of yarn around any stitch to mark Row 2 as **right** side.

Row 3: Ch 3, turn; dc in next dc, (dc, ch 1, dc) in next ch-1 sp, skip next dc, work BPdc around each of next 3 FPtr, (dc, ch 1, dc) in next 23 ch-1 sps, skip next dc, work BPdc around each of next 3 FPtr, (dc, ch 1, dc) in next ch-1 sp, skip next dc, dc in last 2 dc.

Row 4: Ch 3, turn; dc in next dc, (dc, ch 1, dc) in next ch-1 sp, skip next dc, work FPtr around each of next 3 BPdc, (dc, ch 1, dc) in next 23 ch-1 sps, skip next dc, work FPtr around each of next 3 BPdc, (dc, ch 1, dc) in next ch-1 sp, skip next dc, dc in last 2 dc.

Rows 5-18: Repeat Rows 3 and 4, 7 times.

Row 19: Ch 3, turn; dc in next 2 dc, dc in next ch-1 sp and in next dc, work BPtr around each of next 3 FPtr, dc in next dc and in each ch-1 sp and each dc across to next 3 FPtr, work BPtr around each of next 3 FPtr, dc in next dc and in next ch-1 sp, dc in last 3 dc changing to White in last dc ***(Fig. 5a, page 77)***, cut Blue.

Trim: Ch 1, turn; 3 sc in first dc, sc in each st across to last dc, 3 sc in last sc; sc evenly across ends of rows; working in free loops of beginning ch ***(Fig. 3b, page 77)***, 3 sc in marked ch, remove marker, sc in each ch across to last ch, 3 sc in last ch; sc evenly across ends of rows; join with slip st to first sc, finish off.

TAB

With White, ch 13.

Row 1 (Right side)**:** Sc in second ch from hook and in each ch across: 12 sc.

Note: Mark Row 1 as **right** side.

Rows 2 and 3: Ch 1, turn; sc in each sc across.

Finish off.

TIES

With **right** side facing, join White with slip st in end of Row 2 on Tab, ch 51; finish off.

Repeat Tie in opposite end of Row 2.

FINISHING

With **wrong** side together, fold first row and last row to the center of Case to form flaps.

With **right** side facing and White, sew top and bottom edges of flaps.

With **right** side facing and using photo as a guide for placement, sew ends of Tab to middle of Case.

To secure Case, tie Ties in a bow.

General Instructions

ABBREVIATIONS

BPdc	Back Post double crochet(s)
BPtr	Back Post treble crochet(s)
ch(s)	chain(s)
cm	centimeters
dc	double crochet(s)
dc2tog	double crochet 2 together
FPdc	Front Post double crochet(s)
FPtr	Front Post treble crochet(s)
hdc	half double crochet(s)
hdc2tog	half double crochet 2 together
mm	millimeters
Rnd(s)	Round(s)
sc	single crochet(s)
sc2tog	single crochet 2 together
sc3tog	single crochet 3 together
sp(s)	space(s)
st(s)	stitch(es)
tr	treble crochet(s)
YO	yarn over

SYMBOLS & TERMS

★ — work instructions following ★ as many **more** times as indicated in addition to the first time.

( ) or **[ ]** — work enclosed instructions **as many** times as specified by the number immediately following **or** work all enclosed instructions in the stitch or space indicated **or** contains explanatory remarks.

colon (:) — the number(s) given after a colon at the end of a row or round denote(s) the number of stitches and/or spaces you should have on that row or round.

CROCHET TERMINOLOGY

United States		International
slip stitch (slip st)	=	single crochet (sc)
single crochet (sc)	=	double crochet (dc)
half double crochet (hdc)	=	half treble crochet (htr)
double crochet (dc)	=	treble crochet (tr)
treble crochet (tr)	=	double treble crochet (dtr)
double treble crochet (dtr)	=	triple treble crochet (ttr)
triple treble crochet (tr tr)	=	quadruple treble crochet (qtr)
skip	=	miss

CROCHET HOOKS

United States	Metric (mm)	United States	Metric (mm)	United States	Metric (mm)
B-1	2.25	7	4.5	M/N-13	9
C-2	2.75	H-8	5	N/P-15	10
D-3	3.25	I-9	5.5	P/Q	15
E-4	3.5	J-10	6	Q	16
F-5	3.75	K-10½	6.5	S	19
G-6	4	L-11	8		

BASIC	Projects using basic stitches. May include basic increases and decreases.
EASY	Projects may include simple stitch patterns, color work, and/or shaping.
INTERMEDIATE	Projects may include involved stitch patterns, color work, and/or shaping.
COMPLEX	Projects may include complex stitch patterns, color work, and/or shaping using a variety of techniques and stitches simultaneously.

Yarn Weight Symbol & Names	LACE 0	SUPER FINE 1	FINE 2	LIGHT 3	MEDIUM 4	BULKY 5	SUPER BULKY 6	JUMBO 7
Type of Yarns in Category	Fingering, size 10 crochet thread	Sock, Fingering, Baby	Sport, Baby	DK, Light Worsted	Worsted, Afghan, Aran	Chunky, Craft, Rug	Super Bulky, Roving	Jumbo, Roving
Crochet Gauge* Ranges in Single Crochet to 4" (10 cm)	32-42 sts**	21-32 sts	16-20 sts	12-17 sts	11-14 sts	8-11 sts	6-9 sts	5 sts and fewer
Advised Hook Size Range	Steel*** 6 to 8, Regular hook B-1	B-1 to E-4	E-4 to 7	7 to I-9	I-9 to K-10½	K-10½ to M/N-13	M/N-13 to Q	Q and larger

*GUIDELINES ONLY: The chart above reflects the most commonly used gauges and hook sizes for specific yarn categories.

** Lace weight yarns are usually crocheted with larger hooks to create lacy openwork patterns. Accordingly, a gauge range is difficult to determine. Always follow the gauge stated in your pattern.

*** Steel crochet hooks are sized differently from regular hooks–the higher the number, the smaller the hook, which is the reverse of regular hook sizing.

GAUGE

Exact gauge is **essential** for proper size. Before beginning your project, make the sample swatch given in the individual instructions in the yarn and hook specified. After completing the swatch, measure it, counting your stitches and rows/rounds carefully. If your swatch is larger or smaller than specified, **make another, changing hook size to get the correct gauge**. Keep trying until you find the size hook that will give you the specified gauge.

MARKERS

Markers are used to help distinguish the beginning of each round being worked. Place a 2" (5 cm) scrap piece of yarn before the first stitch of each round, moving marker after each round is complete.

JOINING WITH SC

When instructed to join with sc, begin with a slip knot on hook. Insert hook in stitch or space indicated, YO and pull up a loop, YO and draw through both loops on hook.

BACK RIDGE

Work only in loops indicated by arrows ***(Fig. 1)***.

Fig. 1

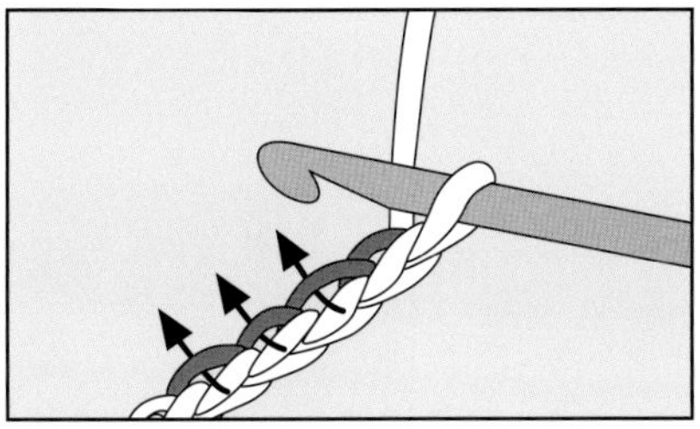

BACK OR FRONT LOOP ONLY

Work only in loop(s) indicated by arrow ***(Fig. 2)***.

Fig. 2

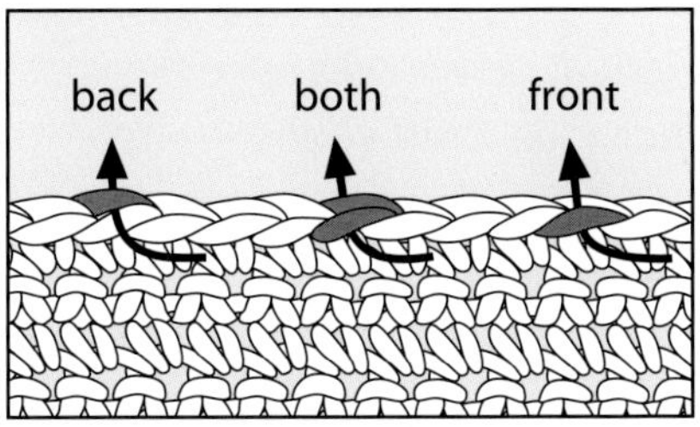

FREE LOOPS

After working in Back or Front Loops Only on a row or round, there will be a ridge of unused loops. These are called the free loops. Later, when instructed to work in the free loops of the same row or round, work in these loops ***(Fig. 3a)***.

When instructed to work in free loops of a chain, work in loop indicated by arrow ***(Fig. 3b)***.

Fig. 3a

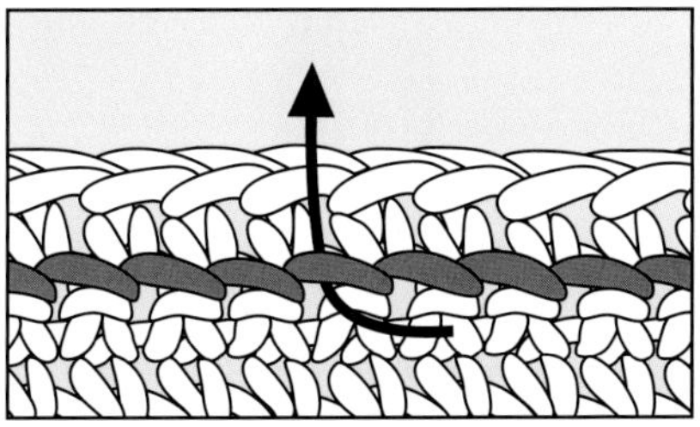

Fig. 3b

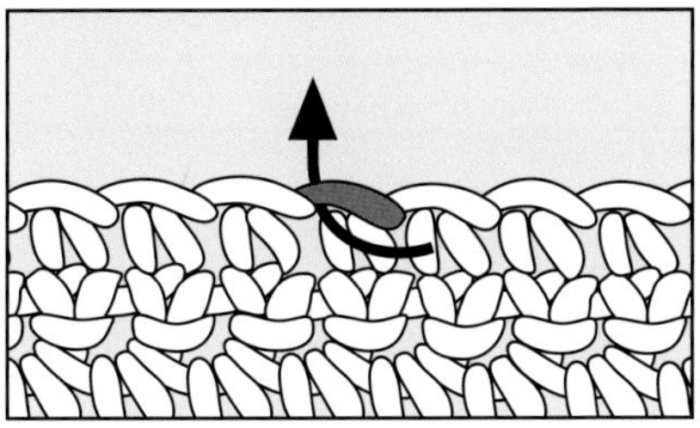

POST STITCH

Work around post of stitch indicated, inserting hook in direction of arrow ***(Fig. 4)***.

Fig. 4

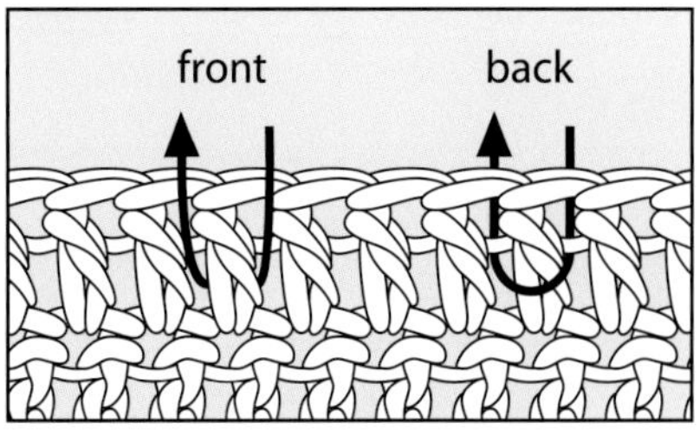

CHANGING COLORS

To change colors at end of a row, work the last stitch to within one step of completion, hook new yarn ***(Fig. 5a)*** and draw through all loops on hook.

Fig. 5a

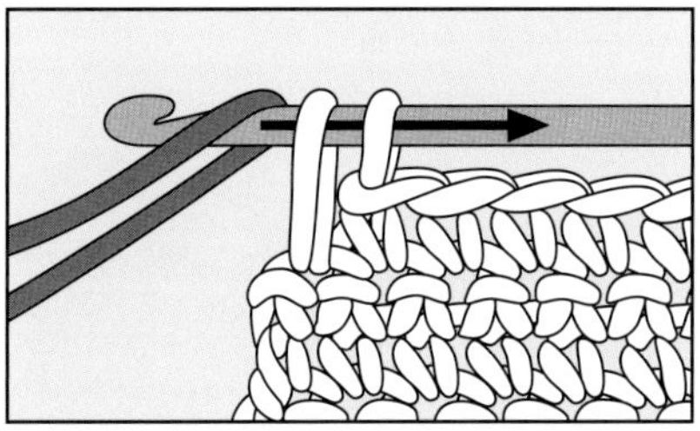

To change colors at end of a round, drop yarn, insert hook in first stitch, hook new yarn and draw through st and loop on hook ***(Fig. 5b)***.

Fig. 5b

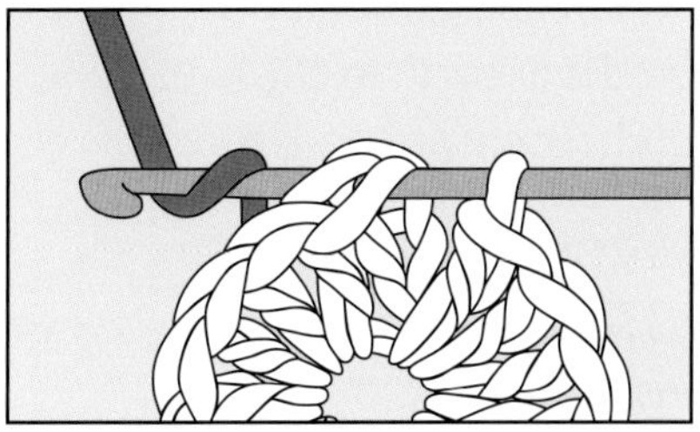

WORKING IN SPACE BEFORE A STITCH

When instructed to work in space **before** a stitch or in spaces **between** stitches, insert hook in space indicated by arrow ***(Fig. 6)***.

Fig. 6

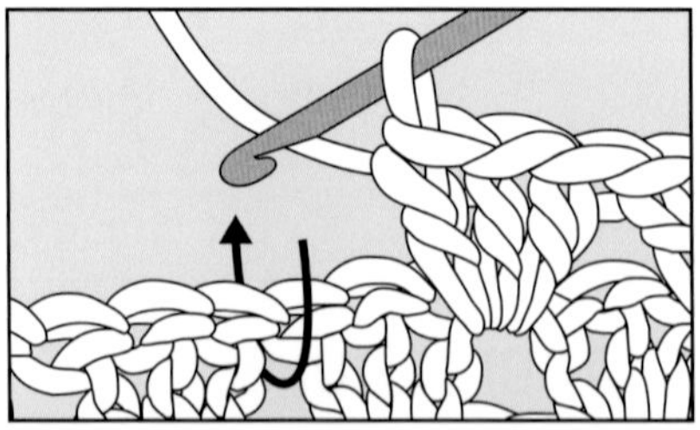

WEAVE THRU STITCHES

Weave yarn end through the stitches ***(Fig. 7)*** and gather to close.

Fig. 7

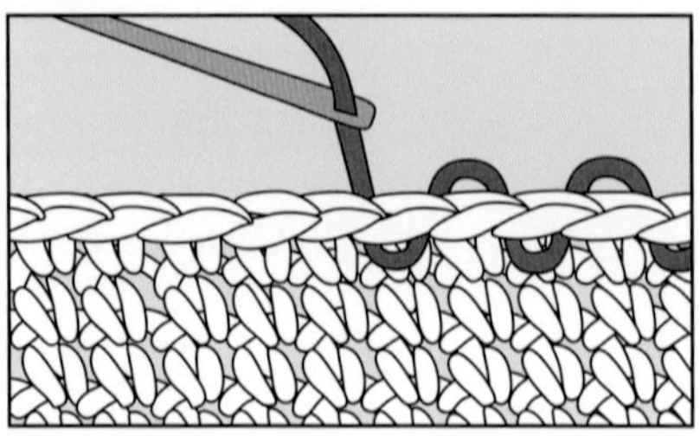

FRINGE

Cut a piece of cardboard 5" (12.5 cm) wide and ½" (12 mm) longer than you want your finished fringe to be. Wind the yarn **loosely** and **evenly** lengthwise around the cardboard until the card is filled, then cut across one end; repeat as needed.

Hold together as many strands as specified in individual instructions; fold in half.

With **wrong** side facing and using a crochet hook, draw the folded end up through a stitch or space and pull the loose ends through the folded end ***(Fig. 8a)***; draw the knot up **tightly** ***(Fig. 8b)***. Repeat, spacing as specified in individual instructions.

Lay flat on a hard surface and trim the ends.

Fig. 8a

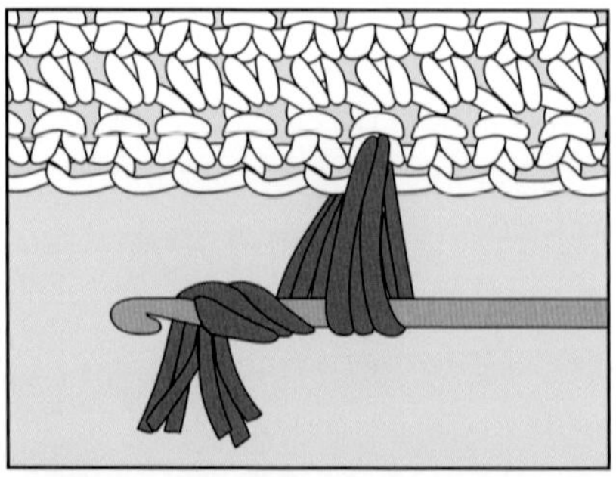

Fig. 8b

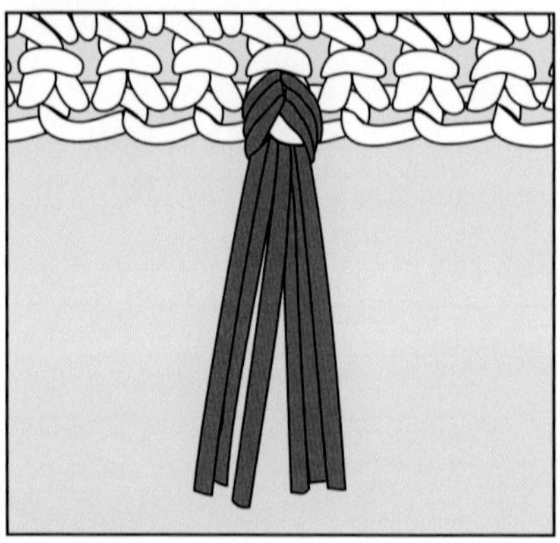

WHIPSTITCH

Place two Squares with **wrong** sides together. Beginning in center sc of corner, sew through both pieces once to secure the beginning of the seam, leaving an ample yarn end to weave in later. Insert the needle from **front** to **back** through **inside** loops only of each stitch on **both** pieces ***(Fig. 9)***. Bring the needle around and insert it from **front** to **back** through next loops of both pieces. Continue in this manner across to next corner sc, keeping the sewing yarn fairly loose.

Fig. 9

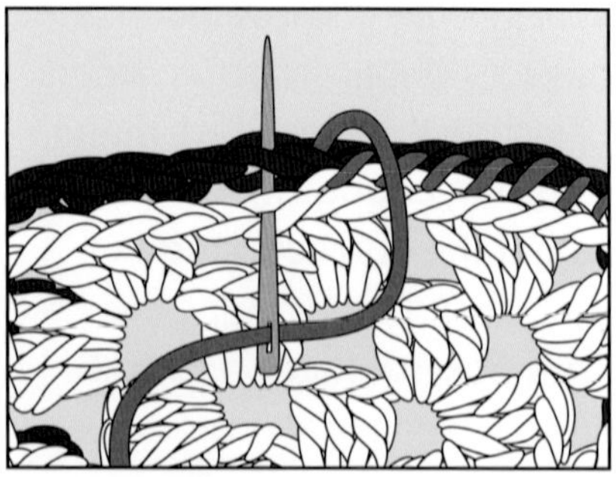

POM-POM

Cut a piece of cardboard 3" (7.5 cm) wide and as long as you want the diameter of your finished pom-pom to be.

Wind the yarn around the cardboard until it is approximately ½" (12 mm) thick in the middle ***(Fig. 10a)***.

Carefully slip the yarn off the cardboard and firmly tie an 18" (45.5 cm) length of yarn around the middle ***(Fig. 10b)***. Leave yarn ends long enough to attach the pom-pom. Cut the loops on both ends and trim the pom-pom into a smooth ball ***(Fig. 10c)***.

Fig. 10a

Fig. 10b

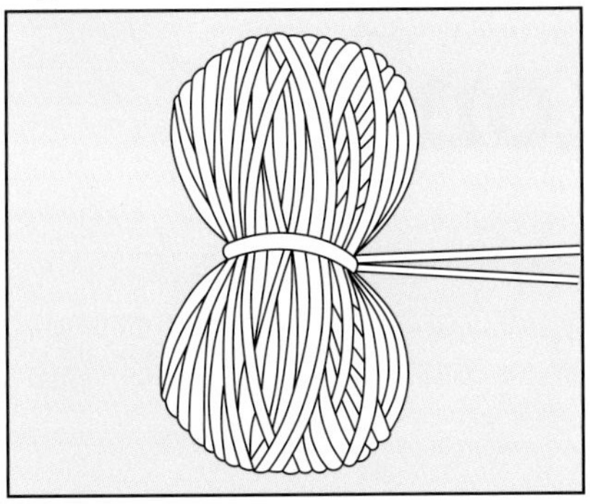

Fig. 10c

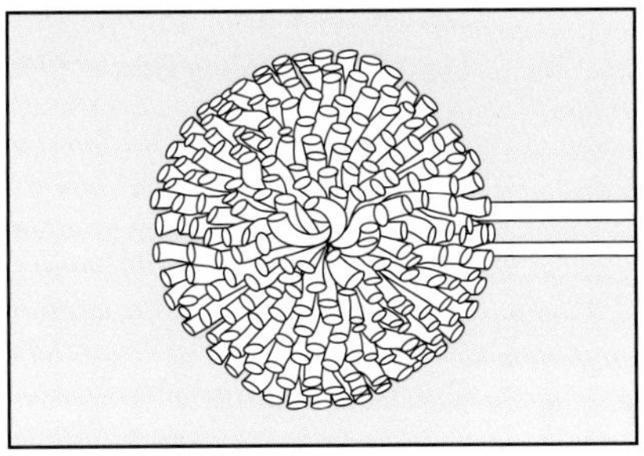

REVERSE SINGLE CROCHET

(abbreviated reverse sc)

Working from **left** to **right**, ★ insert hook in st to right of hook ***(Fig. 11a)***, YO and draw through, under and to left of loop on hook (2 loops on hook) ***(Fig. 11b)***, YO and draw through both loops on hook ***(Fig. 11c)*** **(reverse sc made, *Fig. 11d*)**; repeat from ★ around.

Fig. 11a

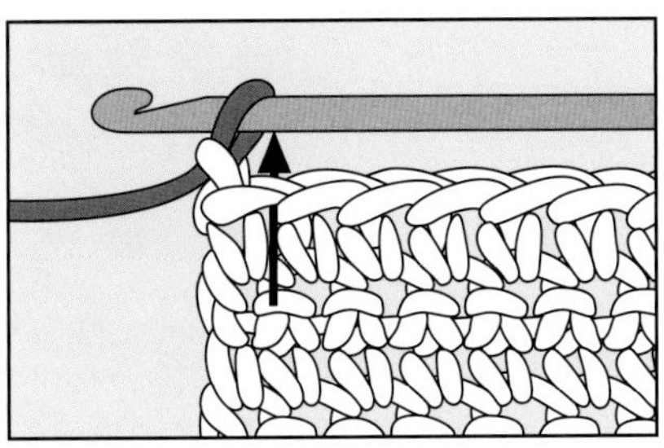

Fig. 11b

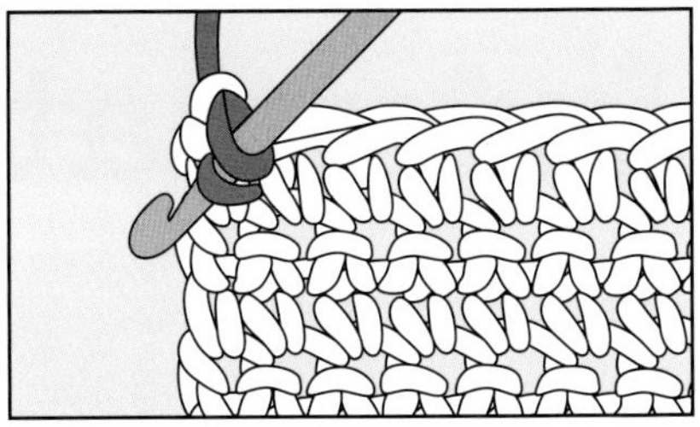

Fig. 11c

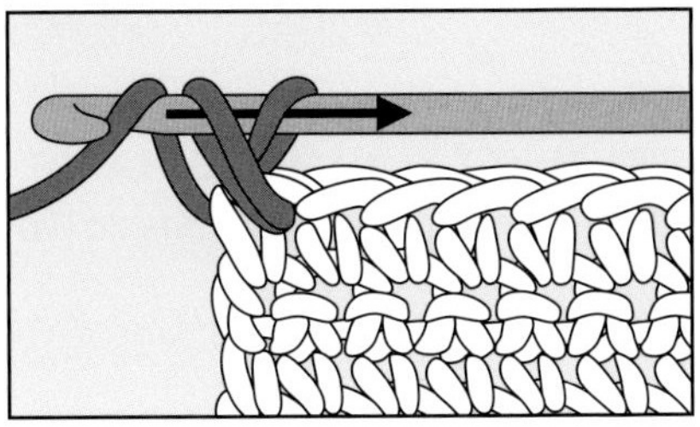

Fig. 11d

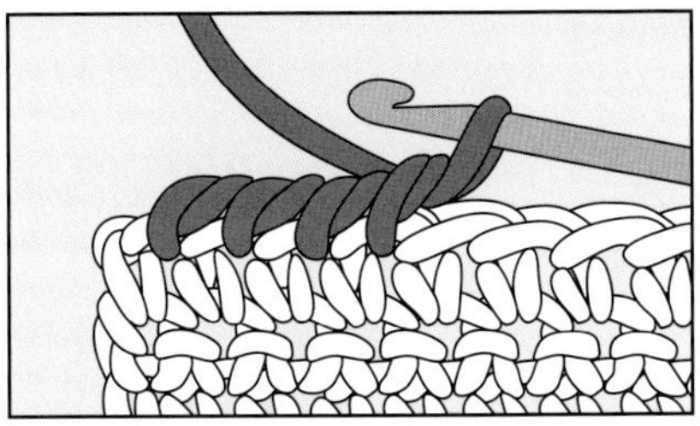

EMBROIDERY STITCHES

SATIN STITCH

Satin stitch is a series of straight stitches worked side by side that come out of and go into the same stitch ***(Fig. 12)***. Come up at odd numbers and go down at even numbers.

Fig. 12

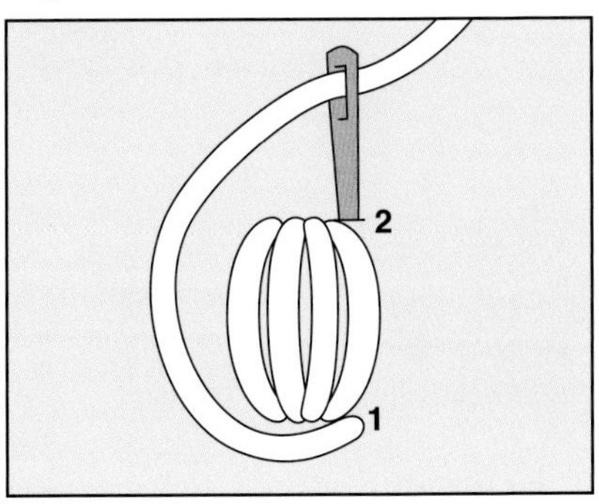

STRAIGHT STITCH

Straight stitch is just what the name implies, a single, straight stitch. Come up at 1 and go down at 2 ***(Fig. 13)***.

Fig. 13

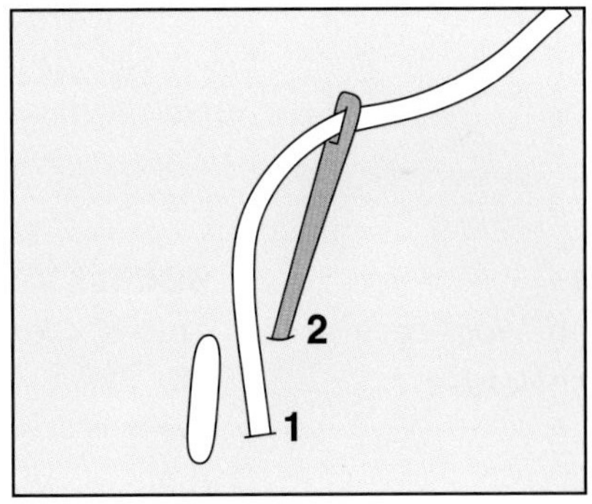

FRENCH KNOT

Bring needle up at 1. Wrap yarn around the needle the desired number of times and insert needle at 2, holding end of yarn with non-stitching fingers ***(Fig. 14)***. Tighten knot; then pull needle through, holding yarn until it must be released.

Fig. 14

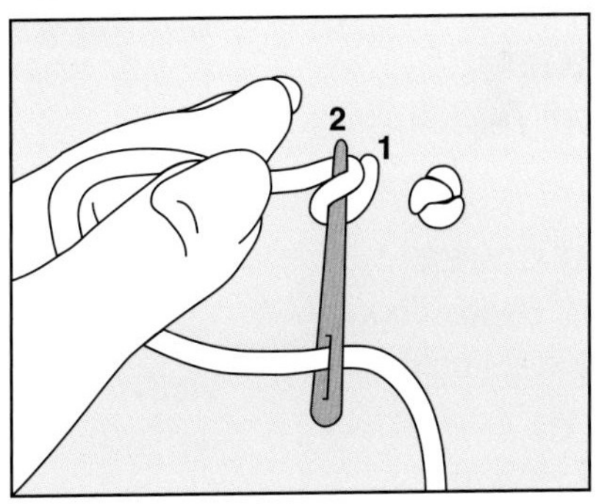

Yarn Information

The items in this book were made using a variety of yarns. Any brand of the specific weight of yarn may be used. It is best to refer to the yardage/meters when determining how many balls or skeins to purchase. Remember, to achieve the same look, it is the weight of yarn that is important, not the brand of yarn.

For your convenience, listed below are the specific yarns used to create our photography models. Because yarn manufacturers make frequent changes to their product lines, you may sometimes find it necessary to use a substitute yarn or to search for the discontinued product at alternate suppliers (locally or online).

BANNER
Lion Brand® Wool-Ease®
#104 Blush Heather

BOOTIES
Premier® Everyday®
Gray - #ED100-23 Mist
White - #ED100-01 White

BUNNY BASKET
Lion Brand® Thick & Quick®
White - #100 White
Gray - #150 Oxford Grey

WHITE & GRAY BLANKET
Red Heart® Hygge Charm™
White - #6311 Stargaze
Gray - #6341 Shooting Star

CHANDELIER
Lion Brand® Thick & Quick®
#100 White

CAR SEAT COVER
Red Heart® Hygge Charm™
White - #6311 Stargaze
Gray - #6341 Shooting Star
Pink - #6724 Meteor
Blue - #6381 Star Blue

BOBBLE STRIPE BLANKET
Patons® Classic Wool Worsted™
Blue - #77115 New Denim
Aran - #00202 Aran

STORAGE BASKET
Premier® Mega Tweed®
#1007-02 Gray Tweed

PILLOW
Lion Brand® Scarfie
#216 Cream/Silver

POUF FOOTSTOOL
Lion Brand® Heartland® Thick & Quick®
#151 Katmai

RASCAL RACCOON
Lion Brand® Vanna's Choice®
Gray - #150 Pale Grey
Black - #153 Black
White - #100 White

RUSTIC THROW
Red Heart® Hygge™
#8319 Rust

LAMB CURTAIN TIE
Patons® Classic Wool Worsted™
Off White - #00201 Winter White
Dark Gray - #00225 Dark Gray Mix
Gray - #00224 Gray Mix

LAMB WALL HANGING
Patons® Classic Wool Worsted
Off White - #00201 Winter White
Green - #77219 Seafoam
Gray - #00224 Gray Mix

SWADDLE COCOON
Red Heart® Hygge™
#8600 Ivy

BUNNY TOY
Red Heart® Hygge Charm™
White - #6311 Stargaze
Gray - #6341 Shooting Star
Pink - #6724 Meteor
Blue - #6381 Star Blue

DEER LOVIE
Lion Brand® New Basic 175™
Tan - #123 Cafe Au Lait
Cream - #098 Cream
Brown - #126 Espresso

OWL MOBILE
Caron® X Pantone™
#01010 River Rock

WOODLAND RUG
Lion Brand® Wool-Ease®
Brown - #403 Mushroom
Gray - #152 Oxford Grey
Cream - #098 Natural Heather

WIPES CASE
Lion Brand® Jeans®
Blue - #150 Vintage
Lion Brand® Vanna's Choice®
White - #100 White

We have made every effort to ensure that these instructions are accurate and complete. We cannot, however, be responsible for human error, typographical mistakes, or variations in individual work.

Production Team: Instructional/Technical Editor-Sarah J. Green; Senior Graphic Artist-Lora Puls; Graphic Artist-Michael Douglas; Photo Stylist-Lori Wenger; and Photographer-Jason Masters.

Library of Congress Control Number:2019943887

Made in U.S.A.